KANJI
POWER

A Workbook
for Mastering
Japanese Characters

John Millen

CHARLES E. TUTTLE COMPANY
Rutland, Vermont & Tokyo, Japan

The publisher would like to thank the Nihon Shodō Kyōkai
for permitting the use of stroke order tables from their publication
Gendai Pen Ji Kōza Jōyō Kanji no Hitsujunhyō.

Published by the Charles E. Tuttle Company, Inc.
of Rutland, Vermont & Tokyo, Japan
with editorial offices
at 2-6 Suido 1-chome, Bunkyo-ku, Tokyo 112

LCC Card No. 92-61822
ISBN 0-8048-1725-1

First edition, 1993
Third printing, 1995

Printed in Japan

Contents

Introduction

This text has been designed for foreign students of Japanese who are interested in developing their proficiency in the reading and writing of *kanji,* or the Chinese characters that are used in written Japanese. Writing Japanese is often thought to be a difficult task. I have always felt that the emphasis on the word *difficult* has tended to give the study of Japanese an unfavorable reputation. Rather than *difficult,* the word that I prefer to associate with the learning of written Japanese is *different.*

Kanji Power describes the first 240 characters of the most commonly used 881 characters, as designated by the Ministry of Education. This is the same number of Chinese characters covered in the first two years of elementary school in Japan.

The book presupposes an acquaintance with the spoken language and a rudimentary knowledge of the patterns and structures of modern spoken Japanese. In addition, it is assumed that the student already has mastered *hiragana* and *katakana,* the two indigenous Japanese syllabaries.

In the text, each entry or target *kanji* appears with its *on* (Chinese) reading written in *katakana,* its *kun* (Japanese) reading in *hiragana,* and its general meaning. Irregular readings are indicated by an asterisk. To assist in the memorization of particular characters, some information regarding derivation has been included. The basic meanings of each character are provided with example sentences to illustrate their usage. It should be noted that no romanization is used in this text. A number of common compounds are listed for each entry in order to introduce as many readings of the target character as possible.

The most important aspect of developing one's reading and writing skills is of course, practice; the student of Japanese must be patient and prepared to devote much time to writing Chinese characters. As the aim of this book is to thoroughly familiarize students with the 240 target characters, it is recommended that one devote a lot of time to writing and using these *kanji* in various contexts. The memorization of *kanji* is in part an intellectual feat, but it is also a manual skill; it is through writing the same basic characters over and over again that stroke order becomes second nature. For this reason, advice on how to write each character and a grid to practice it will also be provided.

A weakness of any text of this nature is that in order to introduce new characters in as many combinations as possible, it becomes necessary to use other unknown characters that may tend to complicate the situation. For this reason, *furigana* is added to facilitate the comprehension of such samples and I think that through repetition and constant exposure, the student might at least gain a passive command of many new characters.

Quizzes appear after each group of six entries, tests follow at intervals of approximately 24 characters, and review tests are given for every 80 *kanji.* Every effort has been made to test each target character in a large variety of contexts. The student is advised to work through the text at a leisurely pace, revising constantly and doing the tests to gauge one's rate of improvement. I hope that by presenting the characters in their graded order and describing them in this systematic fashion, this text will be of some assistance to the student of Japanese wishing to develop *kanji power.*

Introduction

The publication of a work of this kind requires the cooperation and assistance of many people. In particular I would like to express my deep appreciation to Mr. Tsuneharu Kubota and to Mr. Tadaaki Shimizu for their advice and guidance in the compilation of this text. My special thanks also to the Charles E. Tuttle Company for their much-need editorial assistance.

まえがき

　このテキストは漢字の読み書きの力を伸ばしたいと思っている外国人の日本語学習者を対象にしている。とかく日本語を書くことは難しいと思われがちである。それがあまり強調されるために日本語学習そのものが敬遠されてしまう。そこで私はこの「難しい」という言葉のかわりに日本語の読み書きはとても「ちがう」と考えたらいいと思う。

　この*Kanji Power*は教室で適切なテキストの補助教材として理想的であるが、また個人用としても自分のペースで学習し、練習問題やテストによって自己評価ができるようになっている。ローマ字表記に依存することは、この本の目的である読み書きの力を伸ばすことに役立つとは思えないので、この本では採用していない。このテキストは段階を踏んで学習できるようになっているので、教師は学習者の能力に応じてどこからでも始めることができる。つまり個人のペースに合わせて進めることができるのでクラスで家庭学習用に課すこともできるし、また能力差のある様々なグループを教える場合にも対応できるようになっている。この*Kanji Power* が多くのテキストと一緒に採用されることにより，学習者が同じ漢字に様々な使用法があることを知ることが望ましいと思う。

　*Kanji Power*の扱う範囲は文部省指定の教育漢字881字のうち、初歩の240字である。それは大体日本の小学校の一、二年で学習する漢字に相当する。この240字を80字ずつに分け、更に6字毎に分けて、6字学習する毎に練習問題をつけ漢字が系統的に提示されるようにした。読み書きの能力を伸ばすためには練習することが大切なことは勿論である。そこで日本語学習者は充分時間をかけて粘り強く漢字を書くように努めなければならない。漢字を覚えることは一面において知的な作業であるが、また手を使う技能でもある。同じ漢字を何回も実際に書いてみることによって、はじめて書き順が自然に身につくのである。

　いうまでもなく、日本語の書き方に関するどんなテキストにも限界があり、この*Kanji Power*も例外ではない。この本は現代日本語の口語の文型構造についての初歩的な知識を養うことを意図している。学習者はひらがなとカタカナを既に習得しており、「すばらしい漢字の世界」に一歩踏み込んでいることが望ましい。系統的な漢字の学習によって、漢字の知識が確立するように作られている。

　各見出し語、つまり目標漢字にはカタカナで音よみを、ひらがなで訓よみをつけ一般的な意味を示した。変則的な読み方はアステリスク(*)をつけた。特定の文字を覚えるための手助けとして、その漢字の成立ちに関する説明をつけた。各漢字の基本的な意味には、使い方を示す例文をつけた。この例文が読み易いように、このテキストの漢字には全てふりがなをつ

けた。見出し語にはその読み方をできるだけ多く知ってもらうために一般的な熟語がいくつか配してある。最後に、見出し漢字の書き方を練習するためのグリッド（ます目）と、漢字を書く時に注意すべき点についての助言を付してある。

　このテキストの目的は、学習者が目標の240字の漢字に習熟することにあるので、これらの漢字を書き、且つ様々な文脈に入れて用いる練習を充分することをすすめたい。この種のテキストにありがちな弱点として、新しい漢字をできるだけ多くの組み合わせの中で示そうとするあまり、どうしても他の未学習の漢字を使うことになり、全体がわかりにくくなってしまうことがある。それを避けるためにふりがなをつけた。漢字にくりかえし触れることにより、少なくとも読める漢字が増えることが期待できるからである。

　6字ずつ学習したあとに練習問題があり、大体24字毎にテストがある。目標漢字の一つ一つを多種多様な文脈においてテストできるように配慮したつもりである。学習者は、たえず復習し、テストをしてみて上達の程度を自分で測りながら、ゆっくりしたペースでテキストを勉強してほしい。このテキストが「漢字パワー」をつけたいと願っている日本語学習者にとって少しでも役立つことを心から願っている。

First Grade Characters

List of First Grade Characters

1. 一	21. 川	41. 出	61. 耳
2. 二	22. 土	42. 正	62. 見
3. 七	23. 五	43. 生	63. 町
4. 八	24. 六	44. 石	64. 車
5. 九	25. 円	45. 田	65. 村
6. 十	26. 王	46. 白	66. 男
7. 人	27. 火	47. 本	67. 足
8. 入	28. 月	48. 目	68. 赤
9. 力	29. 犬	49. 立	69. 花
10. 三	30. 手	50. 百	70. 貝
11. 千	31. 水	51. 年	71. 学
12. 上	32. 中	52. 気	72. 金
13. 下	33. 日	53. 名	73. 空
14. 大	34. 天	54. 先	74. 青
15. 小	35. 文	55. 早	75. 林
16. 口	36. 木	56. 休	76. 雨
17. 山	37. 四	57. 字	77. 草
18. 子	38. 右	58. 糸	78. 音
19. 女	39. 左	59. 竹	79. 校
20. 夕	40. 玉	60. 虫	80. 森

1

一 イチ、イッ
ひと、ひと・つ
one, first

一, a single line, indicates the number *one*. It also signifies the *beginning* of something.

Example sentences and meanings

1. one

* 一週間に一回学校に行く
to go to school once a week

* コピーを一枚とって。
Make a copy of this!

2. the first

* 電車の一番前に乗る
to ride in the front of the train

3. the best

* そのビルは日本一高い建物だ。
That building is the tallest in Japan.

4. the whole

* 文房具一式を用意する
to prepare a complete set of writing materials

Common compounds

一回	いっかい	once, one time
一年	いちねん	one year
均一	きんいつ	uniformity
一月	いちがつ・ひとつき	January, one month
*一人	ひとり	one person

begin stroke boldly → 一 ← end stroke firmly

1 一

2

二 ニ
ふた、ふた・つ
two

二, two lines, indicates the number *two*.

Example sentences and meanings

1. two

* 明日の午後二時に会いましょう。
Let's meet at 2:00 p.m. tomorrow.

2. the second

* 二月に二人目の子供が生まれる。
My second child will be born in February.

* 日本語検定の二級に受かった。
I passed the second level of the Japanese language examination.

3. to do again, repeatedly

* 二度と同じ過ちを繰り返すな。
Don't make the same mistake again!

Common compounds

二世	にせい	second generation Japanese, the Second (name)
*二人	ふたり	two persons
*二十日	はつか	20 days, 20th day of the month
*二十歳	はたち	20 years of age

二 一 longer than stroke above it

2 一 二

3 七 シチ / なな、なな・つ、*なの / seven

七 represented a bent finger under a fist, an ancient way of signaling *seven*.

Example sentences and meanings

1. seven

* 七月七日は七夕です。
  July 7 is the Tanabata Festival.

2. many

* あの女優は七色の声をもつ。
  That actress can do many different voices.

Common compounds

七五三	しちごさん	festival (November 15) for children aged 3, 5, and 7
七年間	ななねんかん・しちねんかん	seven years
*七日	なのか	seven days, seventh day of the month

七　← stroke ends with hook

2　一 七

七

---

4 八 ハチ、ハツ / や、やつ、*よう、*よつ / eight

八 represents something that can be easily *divided in two*.

Example sentences and meaning

1. eight

* 日本に来て八年になる。
  It has been eight years since I came to Japan.

* 卸し値は八掛けだ。
  The wholesale price is 80 percent (of the retail price).

2. many

* 帰りに八百屋で買い物をする
  to shop at the vegetable store on the way home

* 八方美人はよくない。
  It isn't good to be everybody's friend.

Common compounds

八月	はちがつ	August
八頭身	はっとうしん	well-proportioned figure, beautiful body
*八日	ようか	eight days, eighth day of the month

leave space →　八

2　ノ 八

八

5 九　キュウ、ク
ここの・つ、ここの
nine

九 depicted a bent elbow, an ancient way of indicating the number *nine*.

Example sentences and meaning

1. nine
* 東京まで九時間かかる
to take nine hours to get to Tōkyō

2. many
* 九十九折の坂を登る
to climb a zigzag path up a hill
* 彼は九死に一生をえた。
He narrowly escaped death.

Common compounds

九日　ここのか　nine days, ninth day of the month
九月　くがつ　September
九州　きゅうしゅう　Kyūshū (place)
十中八九　じゅっちゅうはっく　nine cases out of ten, most likely

九 ← stroke ends with hook

2 ノ 九

九

6 十　ジュウ、ジッ
とお、と
ten

一 represents east-west, while ｜ represents north-south; thus, 十 signifies all *directions*. The number *ten* derived from this meaning.

Example sentences and meaning

1. ten
* 旅行は十日間の予定です。
I'm planning a ten-day trip.

2. many
* 食べ物の好みは十人十色だ。
When it comes to food, there are so many people, and so many tastes.

3. complete, perfect
* 準備体操を十分にして下さい。
Don't rush through your warm up.

Common compounds

十分　じゅうぶん　enough, plenty of
十月　じゅうがつ　October
十日　とおか　ten days, tenth day of the month
十分　じっぷん・じゅっぷん　ten minutes

十 ← lower part of stroke longer

2 一 十

十

Quiz 1–7

Quiz 1 (1-6)

A. Write in hiragana

1. 日本一　＿＿＿＿＿＿＿＿＿
2. 一人　＿＿＿＿＿＿＿＿＿
3. 二月　＿＿＿＿＿＿＿＿＿
4. 二級　＿＿＿＿＿＿＿＿＿
5. 七年間　＿＿＿＿＿＿＿＿
6. 八日　＿＿＿＿＿＿＿＿＿
7. 九州　＿＿＿＿＿＿＿＿＿
8. 九時　＿＿＿＿＿＿＿＿＿

C. Write in English

1. 一枚　＿＿＿＿＿＿＿＿＿
2. 二週間　＿＿＿＿＿＿＿＿
3. 二世　＿＿＿＿＿＿＿＿＿
4. 二十二　＿＿＿＿＿＿＿＿
5. 七色の声　＿＿＿＿＿＿＿
6. 八方美人　＿＿＿＿＿＿＿
7. 二十日　＿＿＿＿＿＿＿＿
8. 七夕　＿＿＿＿＿＿＿＿＿

B. Write in kanji

1. いっかい　＿＿回
2. いちねん　＿＿年
3. ふたり　＿＿人
4. はたち　＿＿＿＿歳
5. しちごさん　＿＿五三
6. やおや　＿＿百屋
7. ここのかかん　＿＿日間
8. じゅうがつ　＿＿月
9. にど　＿＿度
10. じゅうぶん　＿＿分

7	人	ジン、ニン ひと man, people	人 represents a side view of a *person*.

Example sentences and meaning

1. **human being, person, people**

* ここは人が多い。
  There are many people here.

2. **other people**

* 人のせいにしないで。
  Don't blame it on somebody else!

3. **counter for people**

* ご家族は何人ですか。
  How many people are there in your family?

4. **kinds of people**

* 妻はドイツ人です。
  My wife is German.

Common compounds

日本人	にほんじん	Japanese person
人気	にんき	popularity
*一人	ひとり	one person, alone
*素人	しろうと	amateur, layman
*仲人	なこうど	go-between, matchmaker

人 don't mistake for 入

keep aligned → 人

2 ノ 人

人

8 入

ニュウ
い・る、はい・る、
い・れる
enter, put in

入 represents the *entrance of a house*.

Example sentences and meaning

1. enter

* 毎晩ふろに入る
to take a bath every evening

* 手術のため入院した。
I checked into the hospital to have an operation.

* 入り口はあそこです。
The entrance is over there.

2. place or keep within certain bounds

* 口座にお金を入れる
to deposit money in an account

* 収入が増えた。
My total income has increased.

Common compounds

記入	きにゅう	entry (in a ledger)
輸入	ゆにゅう	import
入国	にゅうこく	immigration
入学	にゅうがく	admission into school
入社	にゅうしゃ	joining a company

this stroke longer → 入 ← keep aligned

2 ノ 入

入

9 力

リキ、リョク
ちから
power

力 originally represented a *flexed arm*.

Example sentences and meaning

1. power

* 彼には力がある。
He's strong.

2. ability

* 権力を持つ
to possess power or influence

3. to do one's utmost, make efforts

* 目的のために努力する
to strive towards a goal

* 投手は七回まで力投を続けた。
The pitcher continued pitching hard until the seventh inning.

Common compounds

暴力	ぼうりょく	violence
力作	りきさく	masterpiece
力士	りきし	sumo wrestler
実力	じつりょく	competence, ability
協力	きょうりょく	cooperation

stroke tapers off → 力 ← stroke ends with hook

2 フ 力

力

10 三 サン / み、み・つ、みっ・つ / three

三, three horizontal lines, represents the number *three*.

Example sentences and meaning

1. **three**

* 三月三日はひな祭りです。
   さんがつみっか　まつ
   March 3 is the Doll Festival.

* 三角を描く
   さんかく　か
   to draw a triangle

2. **many**

* 再三申し出を断る
   さいさんもう　で　ことわ
   to repeatedly reject an offer

Common compounds

三日	みっか	three days; third day of the month
三ケ月	さんかげつ	three months
三日月	みかづき	new (crescent) moon
三重県	みえけん	Mie Prefecture
*三味線	しゃみせん	shamisen

equal spacing 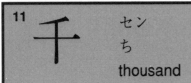 ← this stroke shortest

3	一 二 三

三

11 千 セン / ち / thousand

千 is made up of the characters for イ *person* and 一 *one,* which together represent thousands of people in a crowd.

Example sentences and meaning

1. **thousand**

* その会社は社員数約千人です。
   かいしゃ　しゃいんすうやくせんにん
   There are about one thousand employees in that company.

* 税込み三千九十円です。
   ぜいこ　さんぜんきゅうじゅうえん
   It is ¥3,090, including tax.

2. **very large number**

* 考え方は千差万別だ。
   かんが　かた　せんさばんべつ
   There is an infinite number of viewpoints.

* 知らせを一日千秋の思いで待つ
   し　いちにちせんしゅう　おも　ま
   to wait impatiently for some news

Common compounds

千円札	せんえんさつ	¥1,000 note
一千万	いっせんまん	ten million
千里眼	せんりがん	clairvoyance
千葉県	ちばけん	Chiba Prefecture
千代田区	ちよだく	Chiyoda Ward

千 ← stroke tapers down from right to left

3	ノ 一 千

千

12 上

ジョウ、*ショウ
うえ、かみ、あ・がる、
あ・げる、のぼ・る
above, top, rise, climb

上 was originally written 二, indicating the area *above* a line. The vertical line was added later.

Example sentences and meaning

1. up, above

* 机の上にレポートをおく
to place a report on a desk

2. first part of

* 来年度上半期の予算
budget for the first half of the next year

3. raise, lift up

* 急いで階段を上がる
to hurry up the stairs

4. superior, excellent

* 上等なカシミアのコートを買った。
I bought a high-quality cashmere coat.

Common compounds

値上げ	ねあげ	price hike
向上	こうじょう	improvement
売り上げ	うりあげ	sales
上野	うえの	Ueno (place)
*上手	じょうず	skillful, good at

上 ← vertical stroke does not cross bottom stroke

3 | 丨 卜 上

上

Quiz 2 (7-12)

A. Write in hiragana

1. 仲人 _____
2. 入学 _____
3. 実力 _____
4. 三日月 _____
5. 千円札 _____
6. 千人 _____
7. 権力 _____
8. 入り口 _____

C. Write in kanji and kana

1. German person ___ ___ ___
2. import 輸 ___
3. sales 売 ___ ___ ___
4. Chiyoda Ward ___代田区
5. three months ___ケ月
6. cooperation 協 ___
7. sumo wrestler ___士
8. skillful ___手

B. Write in kanji and kana

1. にゅういん ___ 院
2. どりょく 努 ___
3. みえけん ___ 重県
4. さんぜんえん ___ ___ 円
5. あがる ___ ___ ___
6. うえの ___ 野
7. じょうとう ___ 等
8. なんにん 何 ___
9. さんかく ___ 角
10. にほんじん ___ 本 ___

13 下

カ、ゲ
した、しも、さ・がる、
くだ・る、お・りる
low, below, go down,

下 represents something *below* a vertical line; i.e., something *underneath*.

Example sentences and meaning

1. down, beneath

* 下線を引く
to underline (a word)

2. later time, order

* 七月下旬に夏休みをとる
to take a summer holiday at the end of July

3. low, inferior

* 部下が十人いる。
I have ten people under me.

4. go down

* パソコンが値下がりしている。
The prices of personal computers are dropping.

Common compounds

下着	したぎ	underwear
下さい	ください	please
陛下	へいか	His/Her Majesty
風下	かざしも	downwind
*下手	へた	unskillful, poor at

下 ← end stroke firmly

3 一 丁 下

下

14 大

ダイ、タイ
おお、おお・きい、おお・
きな、お・い
great, important, big

大 depicts a person standing with arms outstretched, suggesting the concept of *big*.

Example sentences and meaning

1. big

* 東京は大きい都市だ。
Tōkyō is a large city.

2. great, important

* 大問題を考える
to consider an important issue

3. many, much

* 大金を持つ
to have a large sum of money

4. abbreviation of 大学 (college)

* 大卒の初任給
the starting salary for a college graduate

Common compounds

大小	だいしょう	large and small
大切	たいせつ	important, precious
大学	だいがく	college, university
最大	さいだい	largest, maximum
*大人	おとな	adult

→ 大 ← strokes taper off

3 一 ナ 大

大

15 小

ショウ
ちい・さい、こ、お
small, little

小 represents a large object being divided into two *small* objects.

Example sentences and meaning

1. small, little

* 小型の車を買う
  to purchase a small car
* 近くの小学校に通う
  to attend a nearby elementary school

2. a little bit

* 小高い丘に登る
  to climb a low hill

3. humble term for my, our

* 明日は小社の創立記念日です。
  Tomorrow is the anniversary of the founding of our company.

Common compounds

小切手	こぎって	check (bank)
小包	こづつみ	parcel, package
小田原	おだわら	Odawara (place)
小山	おやま	Oyama (name)
*小豆	あずき	adzuki bean

note stroke order 小 ← stroke ends with hook

3 | 亅 ⼩ ⼩

小

16 口

コウ、ク
くち
mouth

口 represents the shape of a *mouth*.

Example sentences and meaning

1. mouth

* 口内炎ができて痛い。
  I have a cold sore and it hurts.

2. hole, window, beginning

* 非常口はあそこです。
  Emergency exits are located over there.
* 三時に改札口で待っています。
  I'll be waiting at the ticket gate at 3:00.

3. speaking

* 彼女は早口で話す。
  She's a fast talker.

4. unit for counting people

* 都市に人口が集中する。
  The population is concentrated in the cities.

Common compounds

口紅	くちべに	lipstick
口座	こうざ	bank account
出口	でぐち	exit
大口	おおぐち	big mouth, bragging
辛口	からくち	dry taste, spicy

note stroke order 口

3 | 丨 冂 口

口

17 山

サン
やま
mountain

山 represents the shape of a *mountain*.

Example sentences and meaning

1. **mountain**
   * 富士山に登る
   to climb Mount Fuji
   * 登山が趣味です。
   My hobby is mountain climbing.

2. **things piled together**
   * じゃがいも一山二百円
   two hundred yen for a pile of potatoes

3. **a mine**
   * 父は鉱山の技師でした。
   My father was a mining engineer.

Common compounds

火山	かざん	volcano
山脈	さんみゃく	mountain range
山本	やまもと	Yamamoto (name)
山梨県	やまなしけん	Yamanashi Prefecture

↓↓ same spacing

山

3 ｜ 山 山

山

18 子

シ、*ス
こ
child, baby

子 represents a *baby* with a large head and both arms extended.

Example sentences and meaning

1. **child, baby**
   * 子供が三人いる。
   I have three children.

2. **something separated from the parent**
   * 子会社を作る
   to establish a subsidiary company

3. **egg, seed**
   * たんぽぽの種子が風に飛ばされる。
   The wind blows the dandelion seeds away.

4. **kinds of people**
   * 女子用トイレは二階です。
   The women's toilet is on the second floor.

Common compounds

利子	りし	interest (on a loan)
迷子	まいご	lost child
王子	おうじ	prince
様子	ようす	situation, appearance, state
子孫	しそん	descendant

no break in stroke → 子 ← stroke ends with hook

3 ⁻ 了 子

子

Quiz 3 (13-18)

A. Write in English
1. 下さい _____
2. 七月下旬 _____
3. 大人 _____
4. 小田原 _____
5. 人口 _____
6. 子供 _____
7. 大学 _____
8. 下手 _____

C. Write in hiragana
1. 下線 _____
2. 大切 _____
3. 小切手 _____
4. 非常口 _____
5. 山梨県 _____
6. 様子 _____
7. 口紅 _____
8. 利子 _____

B. Write in kanji and kana
1. だいもんだい ____ 問題
2. へいか 陛 ____
3. しょうがっこう ____ 学校
4. はやくち 早 ____
5. かざん 火 ____
6. まいご 迷 ____
7. こうざ ____ 座
8. かいさつぐち 改札 ____
9. ねさがり 値 ____ ____ ____
10. ふじさん 富士____

---

19 女	ジョ、ニョ、*ニョウ おんな、め woman	女 represents a *woman* with arms and legs bent in a gentle posture.

Example sentences and meaning

1. woman

* その人は女性ですか、男性ですか。
  Is that person a woman or a man?

2. daughter

* 長女は九歳です。
  My eldest daughter is nine years old.

3. weak, the weaker or smaller of two things

* 断られたからといって女々しい態度はしないで。
  Don't go off whining just because you were turned down.

Common compounds

女の子	おんなのこ	girl
男女	だんじょ	men and women
女神	めがみ	goddess
王女	おうじょ	princess
乙女	おとめ	virgin, maiden

note stroke order	女	give character a pentagonlike shape

3 ㄑ 女 女

女

20 夕

セキ
ゆう
evening

夕 depicts the *crescent moon*, viewed during the *evening*.

Example sentences and meaning

1. evening

* 夕焼けで空が真っ赤になる。
  The sky turns bright red with the afterglow of the setting sun.

* 夕食は六時に始まります。
  Dinner will start at 6:00.

* きのう夕刊が来なかった。
  Yesterday's evening paper never came.

* 夕方は忙しい。
  I'm busy in the evening.

Common compounds

夕立ち	ゆうだち	evening squall
夕星	ゆうずつ	Venus
朝夕	あさゆう	morning and evening, day and night
一朝一夕	いっちょういっせき	in one day, overnight

leave gap → 夕

3	ノ ク 夕

夕

21 川

セン
かわ
river

川 represents *flowing water*.

Example sentences and meaning

1. river

* 信濃川は日本で一番長い川です。
  The Shinano River is Japan's longest river.

* 川上は流れが速い。
  The current is swift upstream.

* 河川工事を行う
  to carry out river conservation work

* 川原でバーベキューをする
  to have a barbecue on a dry river bed

Common compounds

小川	おがわ	creek
川柳	せんりゅう	short, humorous verse
川畑	かわばた	Kawabata (name)
川崎	かわさき	Kawasaki (place)
四川	シセン	Sichuan (place)

stroke tapers off → 川   ← center stroke is shortest

3	ノ 川 川

川

22 土

ド、ト
つち

earth, soil, land

土 represents a *seedling* emerging from the *ground*.

Example sentences and meaning

1. soil, earth
* 野菜に付いた土を洗い流す
to wash off the dirt on vegetables

2. land
* 船で本土へ渡る
to go to the mainland by ship
* 東京の土地を買う
to buy some land in Tōkyō

3. abbreviation of 土曜日 (Saturday)
* 土日は休みです。
We have Saturdays and Sundays off.

Common compounds

土木	どぼく	engineering, public works
土器	どき	earthenware
領土	りょうど	territory
土俵	どひょう	the sumo ring
*土産	みやげ	souvenir, present

土 ← this stroke longer than stroke above it

3 一 十 土

土

23 五

ゴ
いつ、いつ・つ

five

In 五 the upper horizontal stroke signifies *ten* and the lower one *one*; the middle line represents *five*.

Example sentences and meaning

1. five
* 五月五日は子供の日です。
May 5 is Children's Day.
* 可能性は五分五分だ。
There's a fifty-fifty chance.
* 五百五十円になります。
That comes to ¥550.

Common compounds

五感	ごかん	the five senses
五月	ごがつ	May
五ケ月	ごかげつ	five months
*五月晴れ	さつきばれ	fine weather during the May rainy season

same spacing ⇄ 五 ← this stroke longer than strokes above it

4 一 丁 五 五

五

24 六	ロク む、む・つ、むっ・つ、*むい six	Although the origins of 六 are not clear, the character now consists of 亠 *roof* and 八 *eight*.

Example sentences and meaning

1. six

* 六月六日の六時に来て下さい。
  Please come at 6:00 on June 6.

* 雪の結晶は六角形です。
  A snow crystal is hexagonal.

* 木にリンゴが六つなりました。
  There are six apples on the tree.

Common compounds

六月	ろくがつ	June
六ケ月	ろっかげつ	six months
第六感	だいろっかん	sixth sense
六本木	ろっぽんぎ	Roppongi (place)
*六日	むいか	six days; sixth day of the month

keep aligned	六	give character a pentagonlike shape

4	一 亠 六 六

六

Test 1 (1-24)

A. Write in kanji

1. princess   王 ___
2. dinner   ___食
3. Kawasaki   ___崎
4. five months   ___ヶ月
5. 6:00   ___時
6. one week   ___週間
7. Tanabata   ___夕
8. October 31   ___月 ___ ___ ___日
9. popularity   ___気
10. ten minutes   ___分

B. Write in hiragana

1. 夕方 _____
2. 五月晴れ _____
3. 第六感 _____
4. 女神 _____
5. 川崎 _____
6. 入国 _____
7. 三角 _____
8. 一千万円 _____
9. 上手 _____
10. 値上げ _____

C. Write in kanji and kana

1. こづつみ   ___包
2. いりぐち   ___ ___ ___
3. とざん   登___
4. おうじ   王___
5. どにち   ___日
6. ごせんえん   ___ ___円
7. むいか   ___日
8. おんなのこ   ___ ___ ___
9. こがいしゃ   ___会社
10. じつりょく   実___

D. Write in English

1. 口座にお金を入れる _____
2. 風呂に入る _____
3. 階段を上がる _____
4. 山を下りる _____
5. 東京大学 _____
6. 七色の声の歌手 _____
7. 女の子が二度来た _____
8. 十一月七日に日本へ行く _____

E. Fill in the kanji and translate

1. （　）での（　焼　）はきれいですね。

2. （　　）さんと（田　）さんではどちらが（　年　）でしょうか。

3. （　田原）で（　型）のトラックを（　台）見ました。

4. （　本木）の（　地）の値段は最近（　）がりましたか。

5. 「お（　産）に何がいいんですか。」
「（　）さい（　形）を（　）さい。」

6. （　月　日）は（　供）の日です。

7. 今（　　）です。

8. （　　）さんにオレンジを（　）つ（　）げました。

9. 「あそこに（　性）が（何　）いますか。」
「（　　）います。」

10. その（　）きい本の（　）に（　　）さんの手紙がありますか。

25 円

エン
まる、まる・い
yen, circle, round

Originally 圓; 囗 is an *enclosure* while 員 represented a *round vessel*. From this came the meaning of a *round enclosure*.

Example sentences and meaning

1. **circle**

* コンパスで円を描く
   to draw a circle with a compass

2. **yen**

* 百六十円の地下鉄の切符を買う
   to buy a ¥160 subway ticket

* 円高が進んでいる。
   The value of the yen has been increasing.

3. **a wide area**

* 関東一円に大雨が降るでしょう。
   Heavy rains are expected throughout the Kantō area.

4. **calm, gentle**

* 年をとってあの人は円くなった。
   He has mellowed as he has become older.

Common compounds

円盤	えんばん	a disc
楕円	だえん	ellipse, oval
円満	えんまん	perfection, harmony
円心	えんしん	center of a circle

end stroke firmly → 円 ← stroke ends with hook

4 丿 冂 冂 円

円

26 王

オウ
king

The three horizontal lines symbolize heaven, earth, and man, and the vertical line represents the person who connects them; namely a *king*.

Example sentences and meaning

1. **king, monarch, ruler**

* 国王は王子のときイギリスに留学した。
   The king went to England to study when he was a prince.

2. **foremost in the field, authority**

* エジソンは発明王といわれている。
   Edison is said to be the "King of Inventors."

3. **king piece is a shōgi game**

* 王手！
   Check! (in Japanese chess)

Common compounds

王様	おうさま	king
女王	じょおう	queen
王族	おうぞく	royal family, royalty
王座	おうざ	throne

→ 王 ⇆ same spacing / this stroke longest

4 一 丁 干 王

王

27 火

カ
ひ、*ほ
fire

火 represents a *blazing flame*.

Example sentences and meaning

1. fire

* ライターの火をつける
  to light a lighter
* 火事を発見する
  to discover a fire

2. abbreviation of 火曜日 (Tuesday)

* 来週の月火は連休だ。
  Next Monday and Tuesday are consecutive holidays.

Common compounds

花火	はなび	fireworks
火山	かざん	volcano
防火	ぼうか	fire prevention, fireproof
点火	てんか	ignite
火薬	かやく	gunpowder, explosives

→ 火 ← strokes taper off

4 丶 丷 ヅ 火

火

28 月

ゲツ、ガツ
つき
moon, month

月 resembles the *crescent moon*.

Example sentences and meaning

1. moon

* 今夜は満月だ。
  There is a full moon tonight.

2. month

* 三ケ月禁煙した。
  I quit smoking for three months.
* 生年月日を書いて下さい。
  Please write your date of birth.

3. abbreviation of 月曜日 (Monday)

* 燃えるごみは月・水・金に出す。
  I put out burnable trash on Mondays, Wednesdays, and Fridays.

Common compounds

先月	せんげつ	last month
今月	こんげつ	this month
月収	げっしゅう	monthly income
正月	しょうがつ	New Year's
毎月	まいつき／まいげつ	every month

same spacing ⇒ 月 ← stroke ends with hook

4 ｊ 几 月 月

月

29 犬

ケン
いぬ
dog

Greatly modified over time, 犬 originally depicted a *dog standing on its hind legs.*

Example sentences and meaning

1. **dog**
   * 番犬を飼う
   to have a watchdog
   * 犬小屋を建てる
   to build a doghouse
   * 子犬が五匹生まれた。
   Five puppies were born.

Common compounds

秋田犬	あきたけん	Akita (dog)
子犬	こいぬ	puppy
狂犬病	きょうけんびょう	rabies
盲導犬	もうどうけん	seeing eye dog

→ 犬 ← strokes taper off

4 一 ナ 大 犬

犬

30 手

シュ
て、*た
hand

手 derived from the shape of a *hand* with its five fingers extended.

Example sentences and meaning

1. **hand, arm**
   * あいさつのとき握手する
   to shake hands when greeting

2. **handmade**
   * あなたの手料理が食べたい。
   I'd like to try some of your home cooking.

3. **way, method**
   * 別の手段を考える
   to think of a different method

4. **personal effects, belongings**
   * やっとほしい本を手に入れた。
   I finally got hold of a book I had wanted.

Common compounds

両手	りょうて	both hands
手間	てま	time and labor it takes to do something
手伝う	てつだう	help, assist
手品	てじな	slight of hand

手 ⇄ equal spacing

4 ' ニ 三 手

手

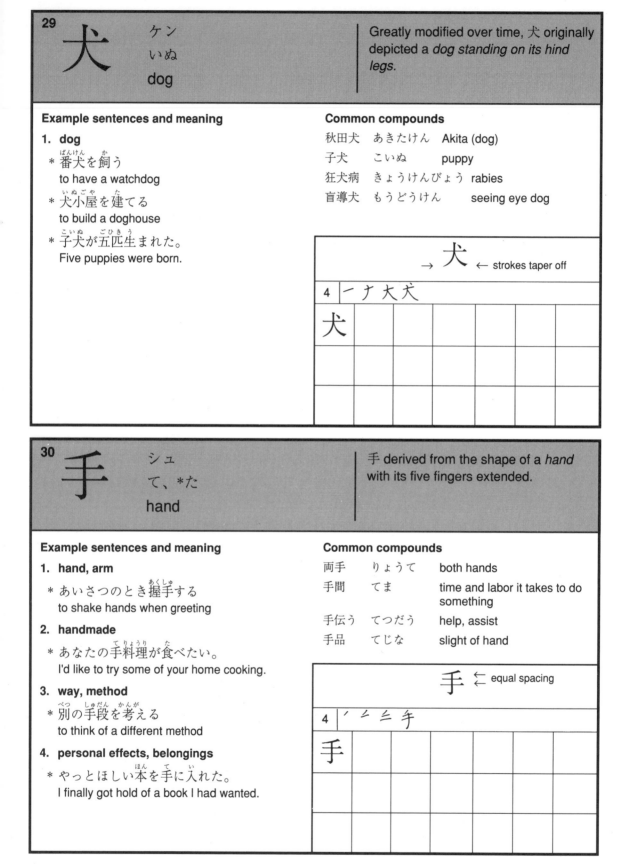

Quiz 4 (25-30)

A. Write in English

1. 円を描く _____
2. 王子 _____
3. 火事 _____
4. 月収 _____
5. 盲導犬 _____
6. 手段 _____
7. 国王 _____
8. 先月 _____

B. Write in hiragana

1. 手伝う _____
2. 秋田犬 _____
3. 正月 _____
4. 防火 _____
5. エリザベス女王 _____
6. 円満 _____
7. 子犬 _____
8. 手料理 _____
9. 点火 _____
10. 九十円の切符_____

C. Write in kanji and kana

1. えんだか ____高
2. おうさま ____様
3. はなび 花 ____
4. さんかげつ ____ケ____
5. いぬごや ____ ____ 屋
6. てにいれる ____ ____ ____ ____
7. こんげつ 今 ____
8. ひをつける ____ ____ ____ ____

31

水

スイ
みず
water

水 represents the *current* and *ripples* of a river.

Example sentences and meaning

1. water, liquid

* 冷たい水が飲みたい。
  I want to drink some cold water.
* 水道代を払う
  to pay the water bill
* 水銀電池を使う
  to use a mercury battery

2. abbreviation of 水曜日 (Wednesday)

* 月・水・金は茶道を習う
  to study the tea ceremony on Mondays, Wednesdays, and Fridays.

Common compounds

水道	すいどう	water supply
水玉	みずたま	drop, dewdrop, dot pattern (on clothes)
水平	すいへい	horizontal
水素	すいそ	hydrogen

note stroke order	水 ← stroke ends with hook
4　丨　ス　水　水	
水	

32 中

チュウ
なか、*じゅう
middle, inside

中 represents an arrow penetrating the *center* of an object.

Example sentences and meaning

1. middle, center

* 駅は街の中心から少しはずれている。
The station is a short distance away from the center of town.

2. inside

* 冷蔵庫の中にビールが入っている。
There's beer in the refrigerator.

3. in the process of, on the way

* 彼は電話中です。
He is on the phone.

4. abbreviation of 中学校 (junior high school)

* 私立中に通う
to attend a private junior high school

Common compounds

途中	とちゅう	on the way, en route
中指	なかゆび	middle finger
中ジョッキ	ちゅうじょっき	medium-size beer mug
*世界中	せかいじゅう	all over the world

中 ↑↑ equal spacing

4	丶	口	口	中			
中							

33 日

ニチ、ジツ
ひ、か
day, sun

日 represents the shape of the *sun*.

Example sentences and meaning

1. the sun

* 日光がまぶしいです。
The sun is very bright.

2. day, daytime

* 締め切りまであと三日しかない。
There are only three days until the deadline.

3. everyday, daily

* 日常会話には困りません。
I have no problems with day-to-day conversation.

4. abbreviation of 日本 (Japan)

* 会議のため来日する
to visit Japan to attend a conference

Common compounds

元日	がんじつ	New Year's Day
日記	にっき	diary, journal
*昨日	きのう・さくじつ	yesterday
*今日	きょう・こんにち	today
*明日	あす・あした・みょうにち	tomorrow

日 ⇐ equal spacing

4	丨	冂	日	日			
日							

34 天　テン　あめ、*あま　heaven

天 combines the characters 一 and 大. 大 represents a *person* while 一 suggests that which is *above* a person, namely *heaven*.

Example sentences and meaning

1. **sky, weather**
   * 今日はいい天気ですね。
   The weather's beautiful today, isn't it?

2. **upper part of something**
   * この部屋は天井が低い。
   The ceiling in this room is low.

3. **nature**
   * この石けんには天然香料が入っている。
   This soap is naturally scented.

4. **by nature**
   * ぼくは天才じゃないよ。
   I'm no genius!

Common compounds

天災	てんさい	natural disaster
天国	てんごく	heaven
天気予報	てんきよほう	weather forecast
天文台	てんもんだい	observatory
天野	あまの	Amano (name)

does not protrude → 天 ← strokes taper off

4　一 二 于 天

天

35 文　ブン、モン　ふみ　letter, sentence, writings

文 derived from a *pattern* used on ancient earthenware. It then took on the meaning of *character,* which then was extended to writing.

Example sentences and meaning

1. **sentence**
   * 彼の文章はわかりにくい。
   His writing is difficult to understand.
   * 例文を考える
   to think of an example sentence

2. **letter**
   * 正しい文字を書く
   to write the correct character

3. **arts, study**
   * エジプト文化に興味を持つ
   to be interested in Egyptian culture

4. **pattern**
   * この文様はきれいです。
   This pattern is pretty.

Common compounds

注文	ちゅうもん	order
文房具	ぶんぼうぐ	stationery items
文学	ぶんがく	literature
作文	さくぶん	composition, writing
文句	もんく	phrase, complaint

this stroke joins → 文 ← strokes taper off

4　丶 一 ナ 文

文

36

木

ボク、モク

き、*こ

tree, wood

木 represents the trunk, branches, and roots of a *tree*.

Example sentences and meaning

1. **tree**
* 桜の木の下でお花見をする
  to enjoy the blossoms while sitting beneath a cherry tree
* 植木に水をやる
  to water a plant or tree

2. **wood, log**
* 木材を輸入する
  to import timber

3. **abbreviation of** 木曜日 **(Thursday)**
* 燃えないごみの日は火・木です。
  Tuesday and Thursday are the days for nonburnable trash.

Common compounds

木造	もくぞう	(made of) wood
木星	もくせい	Jupiter
雑木林	ぞうきばやし	woods
*木の葉	このは	leaves of a tree
*木綿	もめん	cotton (cloth)

→ 木 ← strokes taper off

4 一 十 才 木

木

Quiz 5 (31-36)

A. Write in hiragana

1. 水道代 _____
2. 電話中 _____
3. 日常会話 _____
4. 天井 _____
5. 文字 _____
6. 桜の木 _____
7. 天気予報 _____
8. 中指 _____

C. Match the kanji with its English meaning

1. 水玉 ____
2. 中心 ____
3. 日記 ____
4. 天才 ____
5. 注文 ____
6. 木星 ____
7. 日光 ____
8. 文化 ____

a. genius
b. Jupiter
c. culture
d. order
e. sunlight
f. diary
g. dewdrop
h. center

B. Write in kanji and kana

1. みず ____
2. せかいじゅう 世界____
3. さくじつ 昨____
4. てんごく ____国
5. ぶんがく ____学
6. このは ____ ____葉
7. あす 明____
8. てんもんだい ____ ____台
9. すいようび ____曜____
10. もくざい ____材

37 四
シ
よ、よ・つ、よっ・つ、よん

four

四 originally depicted breath comimg out of a mouth. Some believe that the meaning *four* came from breath spreading out in *all directions*.

Example sentences and meaning

1. four

* 四人で旅行する
to travel in a group of four

* 日本の四季は美しい。
The seasons in Japan are beautiful.

2. the four directions

* ボディガードは四方に気を配る。
The bodyguards are looking out for danger from all directions.

* 四方八方手を尽くして、人を探した。
No stone was left unturned as they searched for the person.

Common compounds

四角	しかく	square
四回	よんかい	four times
四捨五入	ししゃごにゅう	round to the nearest whole number
四国	しこく	Shikoku (place)

stroke inside does not touch → 四 ← stroke bends

5 丨 冂 冂 四 四

四

38 右
ウ、ユウ
みぎ

right

右 combines ナ *right hand* and 口 *mouth*. In the past, people preferred to use their *right hand* for feeding.

Example sentences and meaning

1. right

* 右手をけがした。
I hurt my right hand.

2. superior

* 字のうまさで彼の右に出る者はいない。
When it comes to handwriting skill, he is second to none.

3. assistant

* 彼は社長の右腕だ。
He is the company president's right-hand man.

4. conservative, right-wing

* 右翼の街宣車
right-wing party's (loud-speaker) truck

Common compounds

左右	さゆう	left and right
右利き	みぎきき	right-handed
右目	みぎめ	right eye
右折	うせつ	right turn
右派	うは	right-wing faction

don't mistake for 石   右 ← equal spacing

5 ノ ナ ナ 右 右

右

39 左

サ
ひだり
left

左 combines 𠂇 *left hand* and 工 *work*, and originally meant to help someone at work.

Example sentences and meaning

1. **left**
* 左利きですか。
Are you left-handed?
* 道の左側を車で走る
to drive on the left side of the road

2. **not go well, loss of status**
* 不景気で店が左前になった。
Stores have suffered during the recession.

3. **radical, left-wing**
* 選挙で左派が勝った。
The leftists won the election.

Common compounds

左手	ひだりて	left hand
左折	させつ	left turn
左足	ひだりあし	left leg
左向き	ひだりむき	facing left
左官	さかん	plasterer

don't mistake for 右 左

5 一 ナ た ナ 左

左

---

40 玉

ギョク
たま
jewelry, ball

玉 depicts *jewels* and a *thread* that strings them together.

Example sentences and meaning

1. **jewelry, precious stone**
* 博物館に宝玉のコレクションがある。
There is a gem collection at the museum.

2. **ball, coin, circle**
* 百円玉がポケットの中にあった。
There was a ¥100 coin in my pocket.
* 水玉模様のワンピース
a one-piece dress with polka-dot pattern

Common compounds

珠玉	しゅぎょく	gem, jewel
玉座	ぎょくざ	the throne
玉乗り	たまのり	balancing on a ball
十円玉	じゅうえんだま	¥10 coin

玉 ← this stroke longest

5 一 丁 干 王 玉

玉

41 出

シュツ、＊スイ
で・る、だ・す
go out, take out, send

出 represents a *plant*, thick with leaves, *thrusting upwards*.

Example sentences and meaning

1. **move outside, take out**
   * ＊七時に家を出た。
     I left the house at 7:00.
   * ＊手紙を出す
     to mail a letter
   * ＊自動車を輸出する
     to export cars

2. **appear, display, show**
   * ＊辞書を出版する
     to publish a dictionary

3. **participate in something, appear**
   * ＊会議に出席する
     to attend a conference

Common compounds

出口	でぐち	exit, the way out
外出	がいしゅつ	go out
出前	でまえ	home delivery (from a restaurant)
出張	しゅっちょう	business trip

出
↑ stroke does not protrude

5 ｜ 十 屮 出 出

出

42 正

セイ、ショウ
ただ・しい、まさ・に
correct, just, truly

正 combines 一 *bar* and 止 *leg* to suggest reaching one's destination, or achieving a goal. The quickest way to reach a destination is by going straight; *correct* is a corollary meaning.

Example sentences and meaning

1. **correct, right**
   * ＊重さを正確に量る
     to measure a weight accurately
   * ＊間違いを訂正する
     to correct an error

2. **surely, perfectly, exactly**
   * ＊正にそのとおりです。
     That's certainly right!

3. **originally, main**
   * ＊正面玄関に車を止める
     to park a car at the front of a house

4. **January, beginning of the year**
   * ＊お正月のあいさつをする
     to make one's New Year's greetings

Common compounds

正義	せいぎ	justice
正午	しょうご	noon
正味	しょうみ	net weight
賀正	がしょう	a New Year's greeting
正常	せいじょう	normal

正
← this stroke longest

5 一 丁 下 正 正

正

Quiz 6–43

Quiz 6 (37-42)

A. Write in kanji and kana

1. しほうはっぽう 　＿＿方＿＿方
2. みぎめ 　＿＿目
3. ひだりあし 　＿＿足
4. ごじゅうえんだま 　＿＿ ＿＿ ＿＿ ＿＿
5. でぐち 　＿＿ ＿＿
6. おしょうがつ 　＿＿ ＿＿ ＿＿
7. てがみをだす 　＿＿紙 ＿＿ ＿＿ ＿＿
8. よにん 　＿＿ ＿＿

C. Write in kanji

1. Shikoku 　＿＿国
2. a right turn 　＿＿折
3. a left hand 　＿＿ ＿＿
4. throne 　＿＿座
5. go out 　外＿＿
6. correction 　訂＿＿
7. attendance 　＿＿席
8. left-hand side 　＿＿側

B. Write in hiragana

1. 左右 ＿＿＿＿＿＿＿＿＿＿＿＿＿＿＿＿＿＿
2. 水玉模様 ＿＿＿＿＿＿＿＿＿＿＿＿＿＿＿＿＿
3. 出張 ＿＿＿＿＿＿＿＿＿＿＿＿＿＿＿＿＿＿
4. 正午 ＿＿＿＿＿＿＿＿＿＿＿＿＿＿＿＿＿＿
5. 家を出る ＿＿＿＿＿＿＿＿＿＿＿＿＿＿＿＿
6. 正常 ＿＿＿＿＿＿＿＿＿＿＿＿＿＿＿＿＿＿
7. 左利き ＿＿＿＿＿＿＿＿＿＿＿＿＿＿＿＿＿
8. 四十回 ＿＿＿＿＿＿＿＿＿＿＿＿＿＿＿＿＿
9. 右腕 ＿＿＿＿＿＿＿＿＿＿＿＿＿＿＿＿＿＿
10. 正確 ＿＿＿＿＿＿＿＿＿＿＿＿＿＿＿＿＿＿

---

43 生

セイ、ショウ
う・む、い・きる、は・える、なま

birth, life, grow, raw

生 derived from a pictograph of a *growing plant*.

Example sentences and meaning

1. life

* 祖母は九十歳まで生きた。
 My grandmother lived until age 90.

2. birth

* きのう女の子が生まれた。
 A baby girl was born yesterday.

3. raw, live (performance)

* ジャズの生演奏を聴く
 to listen to a live jazz performance

4. student

* 子供は中学生です。
 My child is a junior high school student.

Common compounds

生ビール	なまビール	draft beer
生け花	いけばな	flower arrangement
先生	せんせい	teacher, doctor
誕生日	たんじょうび	birthday
*芝生	しばふ	lawn

生 ← this stroke longest

5 ノ レ 느 牛 生

生

44 石

セキ、*シャク、*コク
いし
stone

石 depicts *rocks* at the bottom of a cliff.

Example sentences and meaning

1. stone, rock

* 大きな石につまずいた。
I tripped on a large stone.

* 石油を輸入する
to import petroleum

2. lacking in human feelings

* 父は石頭で本当に困る。
My father is so hardheaded, I really don't know what to do.

3. Old unit for measuring rice and saké

* 金沢は百万石の城下町でした。
Kanazawa was a castle town that produced 1 million *koku* of rice.

Common compounds

石炭	せきたん	coal
宝石	ほうせき	precious stone, jewel
一石二鳥	いっせきにちょう	killing two birds with one stone
*磁石	じしゃく	magnet

stroke does not protrude　　石　　don't mistake for 右

5　一 ア 不 石 石

石

45 田

デン
た
rice field, paddy

田 represents an aerial view of a *rice paddy* neatly divided into quarters.

Example sentences and meaning

1. rice fields

* 田に稲の苗を植える
to plant rice seedlings in a paddy

* 水田が道の両側に広がる。
Paddy fields extend on both sides of the road.

* 田植のシーズン
the rice-planting season

2. region with mineral resources

* 海底油田が発見された。
An offshore oil field was discovered.

* 昔ここに塩田があった。
There was once a salt farm here.

Common compounds

田畑	たはた	fields and rice paddies
田園	でんえん	fields and gardens, the country
田村	たむら	Tamura (name)
*田舎	いなか	the country, rural areas

田　make sure character is divided into equal parts

5　l 冂 冂 田 田

田

46 白

ハク、＊ビャク
しろ、しろ・い、＊しら
white

Originally 白 represented the *white nut* of an acorn.

Example sentences and meaning

1. white

＊あの白い車が私のです。
That white car is mine.

2. unblemished, clear

＊私は潔白です。
I am innocent.

3. nothing evident, blank

＊コピーの中に白紙が混ざっている。
There is a blank sheet mixed in with the copies.

4. to speak candidly

＊犯人は犯行を自白した。
The criminal confessed to the crime.

Common compounds

白黒	しろくろ	black-and-white, right or wrong
白人	はくじん	Caucasian
白菜	はくさい	Chinese cabbage
＊白髪	しらが	gray hair

stroke tapers down → 白 ← same spacing
from right to left

5 ノ イ 白 白 白

白

47 本

ホン
もと
book, main, origin

本 represents a *tree* with a *line* marked at the base, suggesting the *most important part*. From this came the meaning *foundation, base*.

Example sentences and meaning

1. book

＊本屋で本を二冊買った。
I bought two books at the bookstore.

2. foundation

＊何でも基本が大事。
Knowing the basics is important for all things.

3. main, head

＊本社は東京にあります。
The head office is in Tōkyō.

4. genuine, real

＊これは本物の金だ。
This is real gold.

Common compounds

日本	にほん	Japan
本州	ほんしゅう	Honshū
本当	ほんとう	true, real
資本	しほん	capital, funds
本日	ほんじつ	today

本
↑ ↑ do not touch

5 一 十 オ 木 本

本

48	目	モク、＊ボク め、＊ま eye	目 represents a human *eye*, turned sideways.

Example sentences and meaning

1. eye

＊目にごみが入った。

I've got a speck of dust in my eye.

2. see, look at, take note

＊大統領に世界中が注目している。

The president is the focus of attention all over the world.

3. target, outlook

＊目的地までの切符を買う

to buy a ticket to one's destination

4. indication of order

＊右から三番目の席に座る

to sit in the third seat from the right

Common compounds

目薬	めぐすり	eye drops
目印	めじるし	mark, sign
目盛り	めもり	scale, degree markings (on a thermometer)

一目惚れ	ひとめぼれ	love at first sight

目 ⊨ equal spacing

5 ｜ 冂 冂 目 目

目

Test 2

Test 2 (1-48)

A. Write in kanji and kana

1. ちゅうがくせい ____学____
2. おおきないし ____ ____ ____
3. すいでん ____ ____
4. はくじん ____ ____
5. ほんじつ ____ ____
6. もくてき ____的
7. はちじゅうななえん ____ ____ ____
8. かざん ____ ____
9. せんげつ 先____
10. ばんけん 番____
11. じょうず ____ ____
12. なまビール ____ ____
13. ほうせき 宝____
14. ほんだ ____ ____
15. しろいくるま ____ ____車

B. Write in hiragana

1. 本州 _____
2. 目印 _____
3. 生け花 _____
4. 一石二鳥 _____
5. 田園 _____
6. 白黒 _____
7. 基本 _____
8. 二番目 _____
9. 水道 _____
10. 途中 _____
11. 三日目 _____
12. 天災 _____
13. 文化 _____
14. 木造 _____
15. 文句 _____

C. Write in English

1. 生け花 _____
2. 石油 _____
3. 田舎 _____
4. 自白する _____
5. 本当 _____
6. 注目 _____
7. 先生 _____
8. 石頭 _____
9. 海底油田 _____
10. 白紙 _____
11. 本物 _____
12. 白菜 _____

13. 四角 _____
14. 右利き _____
15. 左側 _____

D. Match the kanji with its reading

1. 十円玉 ____ a. にほんじん
2. 輸出 ____ b. たんじょうび
3. 正面 ____ c. はなび
4. 誕生日 ____ d. いぬごや
5. 石炭 ____ e. めじるし
6. 田中 ____ f. じゅうえんだま
7. 白髪 ____ g. みかづき
8. 日本人 ____ h. はっせんえん
9. 目印 ____ i. せきたん
10. 八千円 ____ j. ゆしゅつ
11. 発明王 ____ k. げつようび
12. 花火 ____ l. はつめいおう
13. 三日月 ____ m. しらが
14. 月曜日 ____ n. しょうめん
15. 犬小屋 ____ o. たなか

E. Rewrite using as many kanji as possible

1. にほん で うまれた。

   _____

2. いしかわさん の おおきな くち

   _____

3. かわぐちさん の いなか の いえ

   _____

4. しろくろ の テレビ を うって ください。

   _____

5. ほんしゃ は やまぐちけん に ある。

   _____

6. ひとりめ の こども

   _____

7. きゅうひゃくえん の ほん を かった。

   _____

8. さんがい で かじ が おきた。

   _____

9. こんげつ は なんがつ ですか。

   _____

10. てま が かかります ね。

_____

11. この とけい は すいぎんでんち を つかう。

_____

12. なま ビール の ちゅう ジョッキ

_____

13. きょう は いしだくん の たんじょうび だ。

_____

14. この まち は てんごく だ。

_____

15. にほんご の テキスト

_____

F. Fill in the kanji and translate

1. (かわだ) さんの (しろ) い (いぬ) に (ひだりて)
   を かまれた。

2. (こ) どもが (ごにん) (みず) の (なか) から
   (いし) を ひろって (で) きた。

3. (よ) つかどを (みぎ) に まがると (おお) き
   な (てんもんだい 台) が あります。

4. (たなか) さんの ところに (こいぬ) が (う)
   まれたそうです。

5. (ごじゅうえんだま) が (はち) まいで (百えん) のも
   のが (よっ) つかえます。

6. (やまかじ 事) の あとで (き) が なかなか
   (は) えて こなかった。

7. (ちい) さな (おうじょ) さまの (め) は (おお)
   きくて かわいい。

8. (つき) の (なか) に (い) きものが すんでい
   ると (にほん) では いわれています。

9. (ゆうがた 方) に なると (やま) の むこうに ほしが
   みえてきます。

10. (ろくばん 番) の (でぐち) を とおって (ななばん 番) の
    (いりぐち) から (はい) って (くだ) さい。

49 立

リツ
た・つ、た・てる
stand, raise

立 depicts a *person standing* with outstretched arms.

Example sentences and meaning

1. stand upright

* 危険ですから、ここに立たないで下さい。
Please don't stand here, it's dangerous.

2. be formed, realized

* アメリカはイギリスから独立した。
America gained independence from England.

3. form, determine

* 国立大学に入る
to enter a national university

4. occur, begin

* 今日は立春だ。
Today is the first day of spring.

Common compounds

中立	ちゅうりつ	neutrality
対立	たいりつ	confrontation
立体	りったい	three-dimensional
立派	りっぱ	splendid, magnificent
両立	りょうりつ	coexist, be compatible

strokes slant inward → 立 ←

5 | 丶 亠 亣 立 立

立

50 百

ヒャク
もも
hundred

百 combines *one* 一 and *white* 白. It is believed that 白 also once indicated *hundred*; adding 一 thus meant *one hundred*.

Example sentences and meaning

1. one hundred

* 自動販売機に百円玉を入れる
to put a ¥100 coin into a vending machine

* パーティーに三百人ぐらいの人が来た。
About three hundred people came to the party.

2. many, a lot

* 百科辞典で調べる
to look something up in an encyclopedia

* 百聞は一見にしかず。
A picture is worth a thousand words.

Common compounds

百個	ひゃっこ	one hundred pieces
嘘八百	うそはっぴゃく	a pack of lies
百発百中	ひゃっぱつ	always correct, infallible
	ひゃくちゅう	
*八百屋	やおや	vegetable store

stroke tapers down → 百 ⇐ equal spacing
from right to left

6 | 一 ア 丆 百 盲 百

百

51 **年**

ネン
とし
year

年 combines 禾 *rice plant* and 𠆢 person *bent over*. This represented *harvest,* which occurred *every year.*

Example sentences and meaning

1. **year**

＊ 日本に来てから一年たちました。
One year has passed since I came to Japan.

＊ 今年の秋インドに旅行する予定です。
I'm planning to travel to India this fall.

2. **a length of time**

＊ 今60年代が注目されている。
Now everyone is interested in the 60's.

＊ 近年日本に住んでいる外国人が増えてきた。
The number of foreigners living in Japan has been growing in recent years.

3. **age**

＊ 犠牲者は十五才の少年だった。
The victim was a 15-year-old boy.

Common compounds

去年	きょねん	last year
年収	ねんしゅう	annual income
定年	ていねん	retirement age
年賀状	ねんがじょう	New Year's card

stroke is straight → 年

6 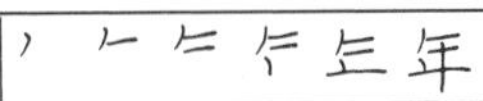

年

52 **気**

キ、ケ
spirit, mind, heart

気 combines メ, which symbolizes *rice,* and 气, which represents the *steam* emitted when rice is cooked.

Example sentences and meaning

1. **weather**

＊ 毎日天気が悪いですね。
Every day the weather is bad, isn't it?

2. **gas, air vapor**

＊ この高原は空気がきれいだ。
On this plateau the air is clean.

3. **feeling, temperament**

＊ 気をつけてね。
Take care!

4. **state of affairs**

＊ だんだん景気が良くなってきた。
Gradually business has picked up.

Common compounds

病気	びょうき	sickness, to be ill
気力	きりょく	energy, vitality
気圧	きあつ	atmospheric pressure
短気	たんき	short temper
電気	でんき	electricity

気 ← stroke ends with hook

6 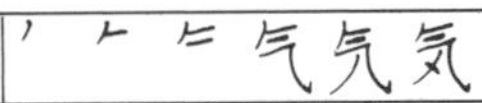

気

53 名

メイ、ミョウ
な
name, famous

名 combines 夕 *evening* and 口 *mouth*. People at night would announce themselves to others by calling out their *names*.

Example sentences and meaning

1. name

* カタカナで名前を書く
to write one's name in katakana

2. fame

* かれはベストセラーを書いて有名になった。
He wrote a bestseller and became well-known.

3. counter for people

* レストランに八名で予約した。
I made a reservation for eight at the restaurant.

4. abbreviation of 名古屋 (Nagoya)

* 東名高速を走る
to drive along the Tōmei (Tōkyō-Nagoya) Expressway

Common compounds

氏名	しめい	full name
名刺	めいし	business card
名産	めいさん	noted product, specialty
名医	めいい	famous doctor
名字	みょうじ	surname

make this stroke long → 名

6 ノ ク タ タ 名 名

名

54 先

セン
さき
previous, ahead, future

先 combines *foot* 生 and *leg* 儿 to give the idea of a person *going foward*.

Example sentences and meaning

1. forefront, first, ahead

* 先着順で受け付ける
to be accepted on a first-come, first-serve basis

* お先にどうぞ。
Please go ahead of me.

2. after a certain time, the future

* あの人は先見の明があるね。
He is good at anticipating things.

3. the past, former

* 先月ロンドンに出張した。
I went to London last month on a business trip.

Common compounds

先生	せんせい	teacher, doctor
先住	せんじゅう	former occupant
先輩	せんぱい	one's senior, superior
優先	ゆうせん	priority, preference
先日	せんじつ	the other day

先 ← stroke ends with hook

6 ノ ト 牛 生 牛 先

先

Quiz 7 (49-54)

A. Write in kanji

1. national university 国 ＿＿ ＿＿学
2. ¥500 coin ＿＿ ＿＿ ＿＿ ＿＿
3. last year 去＿＿
4. electricity 電＿＿
5. Nagoya ＿＿古屋
6. the other day ＿＿ ＿＿
7. vegetable store ＿＿ ＿＿屋
8. retirement age 定＿＿

B. Write in kanji and kana

1. びょうき 病＿＿
2. なまえ ＿＿前
3. せんせい ＿＿ ＿＿
4. たいりつ 対＿＿
5. さんびゃくにん ＿＿ ＿＿ ＿＿
6. しょうねん 少＿＿
7. きあつ ＿＿圧
8. めいし ＿＿刺
9. おさきに ＿＿ ＿＿ ＿＿
10. せんげつ ＿＿ ＿＿

C. Write in English

1. 独立 ＿＿＿＿＿＿
2. 百科事典 ＿＿＿＿＿＿
3. 50年代 ＿＿＿＿＿＿
4. 短気 ＿＿＿＿＿＿
5. 有名 ＿＿＿＿＿＿
6. 先輩 ＿＿＿＿＿＿
7. 名字 ＿＿＿＿＿＿
8. 年収 ＿＿＿＿＿＿

---

55 早

ソウ、＊サッ
はや・い、はや・める
early, accelerate

早 depicted a *rising sun*, from which the meaning of *early* derived.

Example sentences and meaning

1. early, premature

＊夕食にはまだ早い。
It's still too early for dinner.

＊早朝ジョギングする
to jog early in the morning

＊早起きする
to get up early

2. hasten, accelerate

＊早くしなさい。
Hurry up!

＊彼は早熟な子供と言われている。
They say he's a precocious child.

Common compounds

早期	そうき	early phase
早番	はやばん	early shift
早口	はやくち	fast talking
足早	あしばや	quick, light-footed
早川	はやかわ	Hayakawa (name)

equal spacing ⇉ 早

6　丶 丆 𠃌 日 旦 早

早

56 休

キュウ
やす・む、やす・める、
やす・まる
rest, feel at ease

休 combines イ *person* and 木 *tree*, representing a person resting against a *tree*.

Example sentences and meaning

1. rest, stop work

* ちょっと一休みしましょう。
  Let's have a break.
* 休日はテニスをします。
  I play tennis on my days off.
* あのカメラ屋は年中無休だ。
  That camera store is open every day of the year.
* あのデパートは月曜日が定休日です。
  That department store is closed on Mondays.

Common compounds

休養	きゅうよう	recreation
連休	れんきゅう	consecutive holidays
休憩	きゅうけい	a break, intermission
夏休み	なつやすみ	summer holiday
本日休業	ほんじつきゅうぎょう	closed today

→ 休 ← side strokes of 木 taper off

6 ノ イ 亻 什 仕 休

休

57 字

ジ
character, letter

字, which combines *house* 宀 and *child* 子, can be thought of as a child in a house who is studying *characters*.

Example sentences and meaning

1. letter, character

* 映画の字幕を読む
  to read the subtitles of a movie
* 盲人のための点字
  Braille for the blind
* 名字を先に書いて下さい。
  Please write your surname first.
* 漢字は表意文字です。
  Chinese characters are ideographic.

Common compouds

字典	じてん	character dictionary
赤字	あかじ	deficit, in the red
黒字	くろじ	in the black
数字	すうじ	figure, numeral
赤十字	せきじゅうじ	Red Cross

字
stroke ends with hook →

6 丶 宀 宀 字 字 字

字

58 糸

シ
いと
thread

Originally 絲; this character represents a double-stranded *thread*.

Example sentences and meaning

1. thread

* 針と糸、持ってない？
Do you have a needle and thread?

* 白い毛糸のセーター
a white, woollen sweater

2. threadlike things

* なっとうは糸を引くから嫌いだ。
I dislike *nattō* (fermented soybeans) because of its gooey threads.

* 彼は裏で糸を引いているらしい。
He seems to be manipulating things behind the scenes.

Common compounds

絹糸	きぬいと	silk thread
凧糸	たこいと	kite string
糸口	いとぐち	beginning, clue
糸偏	いとへん	*ito,* radical of a Chinese character

single stroke → 糸 ← single stroke

6 ⟨ 幺 幺 糸 糸 糸

糸

---

59 竹

チク
たけ
bamboo

竹 represents a growing *bamboo*.

Example sentences and meaning

1. bamboo

* お祝いには松竹梅がつきものだ。
Pine, bamboo, and plum are associated with celebrations.

* 彼は竹を割ったようなさっぱりした性格だ。
He has a candid, straightforward personality.

* スペインチームは破竹の勢いで連勝した。
The Spanish team won victory after victory, gaining momentum as they went.

* 剣道の竹刀
a kendō bamboo sword

Common compounds

青竹	あおだけ	green bamboo
竹串	たけぐし	bamboo skewer
竹薮	たけやぶ	bamboo thicket
爆竹	ばくちく	firecracker
竹の子	たけのこ	bamboo shoots

end stroke firmly → 竹 ← stroke ends with hook

6 ノ ト ケ 竹 竹 竹

竹

60

虫

チュウ
むし

insect

虫 originally depicted a cobralike *snake* partially coiled up. In the past snakes and insects were grouped together.

Example sentences and meaning

1. bug, insect

* 子供の頃から昆虫に興味があった。

I've been interested in insects since my childhood.

2. mind, feeling, thought

* 今日はボスの虫の居所が悪い。

The boss got up on the wrong side of the bed today.

3. suffix expressing contempt

* なき虫はきらいよ。

I hate crybabies.

4. a person keen on something, a mania

* うちの本の虫は、一日中図書館にいる。

Our bookworm spends all day in the library.

Common compounds

虫眼鏡	むしめがね	magnifying glass
害虫	がいちゅう	harmful insect, pest
防虫剤	ぼうちゅうざい	insecticide
爬虫類	はちゅうるい	reptiles
南京虫	なんきんむし	bedbug

虫 ← end stroke firmly

6 ｜ 丨 冂 口 中 虫 虫

Quiz 8 (55-60)

A Write in hiragana

1. 早起き _____
2. 一休み _____
3. 漢字 _____
4. 毛糸 _____
5. 竹の子 _____
6. 虫眼鏡 _____
7. 赤字 _____
8. 休憩 _____

B. Write in English

1. 早口 _____
2. 連休 _____
3. 字幕 _____
4. 絹糸 _____
5. 竹刀 _____
6. 爬虫類 _____
7. 足早 _____
8. 休日 _____
9. 数字 _____
10. 糸口 _____

C. Match the kanji with its reading

1.	早番	___	a.	みょうじ
2.	定休日	___	b.	いとへん
3.	名字	___	c.	なつやすみ
4.	糸偏	___	d.	ていきゅうび
5.	爆竹	___	e.	がいちゅう
6.	害虫	___	f.	くろじ
7.	黒字	___	g.	はやばん
8.	夏休み	___	h.	ばくちく

61 耳

ジ
みみ
ear

耳 depicts the shape of an *ear*.

Example sentences and meaning

1. ear

* 耳に水が入った。
Some water got into my ear.

2. hearing, hearing ability

* 祖父は少し耳が遠い。
My grandfather is a little hard of hearing.

* それは初耳だよ。
That's the first I've heard of it!

3. handle, edge

* パンの耳を切り落とさないで。
Don't cut the crust off the bread!

Common compounds

耳鼻科	じびか	ear, nose, throat doctor
耳たぶ	みみたぶ	earlobe
耳かき	みみかき	earpick
耳鳴り	みみなり	ringing in the ears
中耳炎	ちゅうじえん	middle ear infection

equal spacing ⇒ 耳 ← end stroke firmly

6 一 丁 F F 巨 耳

耳

62 見

ケン
み・る、み・せる
see, show

見 combines the characters for *eye* 目 and *person* 人, and represents a person *looking* with his eyes.

Example sentences and meaning

1. see, show

* 定期券を見せる
to show one's commuter pass

2. thought, idea

* 自分の意見を言う
to express one's own opinion

* 見方を変える
to change one's outlook

3. appear, show oneself

* 行方不明の美術品が発見された。
The missing artwork was found.

4. meeting a person

* 首相は記者会見した。
The prime minister held a press conference.

Common compounds

見本	みほん	sample, specimen
見当	けんとう	guess, estimate
発見	はっけん	discovery
花見	はなみ	cherry-blossom viewing
見物	けんぶつ	sightseeing

equal spacing ⇒ 見 ← stroke ends with hook

7 丨 冂 冂 月 目 貝 見

見

63 町

チョウ
まち

town, city

町 combines 田 *rice paddy* and 丁 *step* to mean edge of the rice fields—the place where people walk around.

Example sentences and meaning

1. **town, city**

* この町は便利だ。
  This is a convenient town.

* 先日、町長選挙があった。
  The election for town mayor took place the other day.

2. **regional division, name of a town**

* 新しい家は南町三丁目です。
  Our new house is in Minamichō three chōme.

* 本町通りの喫茶店
  a coffee shop on Honmachi Street

Common compounds

町並み	まちなみ	row of stores and houses
田舎町	いなかまち	country town
町会	ちょうかい	town council
港町	みなとまち	port city
町役場	まちやくば	town governmental office

町 ← stroke ends with hook

7　｜　丁　川　田　田　町ー　町

町

64 車

シャ
くるま

vehicle, car

車 depicts the two wheels and carriage of a *palanquin* viewed from above.

Example sentences and meaning

1. **car, train**

* 車庫から車を出す
  to take the car out of the garage

* ここは駐車禁止です。
  No parking here.

* 前から三両目の車両に乗る
  to ride in the third train car from the front

2. **like a vehicle or wheel**

* 小川に水車がある。
  There is a water wheel at the stream.

Common compounds

自動車	じどうしゃ	automobile
電車	でんしゃ	streetcar, train
下車	げしゃ	get off a train or bus
発車	はっしゃ	start, departure (of a train)
車座	くるまざ	sitting in a circle

車 ← this stroke longest

7　一　〒　行　后　百　亘　車

車

65 村　ソン　むら　village

村 combines *tree* 木 and *measure* 寸, and can be thought of as measuring wood to make buildings for a *village*.

Example sentences and meaning

1. village

* 僕は小さな漁村で育った。
 I was raised in a small fishing village.

* 農村の過疎化
 depopulation of rural communities

* 村上さんは村長でした。
 Mr. Murakami used to be the village leader.

Common compounds

村人	むらびと	villager
村道	そんどう	village road
無医村	むいそん	village without a doctor
村八分	むらはちぶ	ostracism
中村	なかむら	Nakamura (name)

this stroke longer than opposite side → 村 ← stroke ends with hook

7 一 十 オ 才 木 朾 村村

村

66 男　ダン、ナン　おとこ、*お　man, male

男 combines characters for 田 *rice paddy* and 力 *strength* and indicates a *man* working.

Example sentences and meaning

1. man, male

* あの背の高い男の人は誰？
 Who is that tall man?

* 男性用のかつらがよく売れている。
 Wigs for men are selling well.

* 歌舞伎は男優ばかりの劇です。
 Kabuki is a form of drama involving only male actors.

2. son

* 長男とは結婚したくないわ。
 I don't want to marry an eldest son!

3. larger of a pair

* こちらが男滝です。
 This is the larger waterfall (of the two).

Common compounds

男子	だんし	man, male, boy
大男	おおおとこ	tall or large man
次男	じなん	second son

equal spacing ⇉ 男 ← stroke ends with hook

7 丨 冂 冂 冊 田 甼 男

男

Quiz 9 (61-66)

A. Write in kanji and kana

1. みみなり ＿＿＿鳴＿＿＿
2. はっけん 発＿＿＿
3. みなとまち 港＿＿＿
4. でんしゃ 電＿＿＿
5. なかむら ＿＿＿ ＿＿＿
6. おとこのこ ＿＿＿ ＿＿＿ ＿＿＿
7. みほん ＿＿＿ ＿＿＿
8. いなかまち ＿＿＿舎＿＿＿

B. Write in hiragana

1. 耳鼻科 ＿＿＿＿＿＿＿＿＿
2. 意見 ＿＿＿＿＿＿＿＿＿
3. 町長選挙 ＿＿＿＿＿＿＿＿＿
4. 駐車禁止 ＿＿＿＿＿＿＿＿＿
5. 漁村 ＿＿＿＿＿＿＿＿＿
6. 男性用 ＿＿＿＿＿＿＿＿＿
7. 耳が遠い ＿＿＿＿＿＿＿＿＿
8. 記者会見 ＿＿＿＿＿＿＿＿＿
9. 自動車 ＿＿＿＿＿＿＿＿＿
10. 無医村 ＿＿＿＿＿＿＿＿＿

C. Write in English

1. 初耳 ＿＿＿＿＿＿＿＿＿
2. 見せる ＿＿＿＿＿＿＿＿＿
3. 町並み ＿＿＿＿＿＿＿＿＿
4. 発車 ＿＿＿＿＿＿＿＿＿
5. 村人 ＿＿＿＿＿＿＿＿＿
6. 長男 ＿＿＿＿＿＿＿＿＿
7. 男子 ＿＿＿＿＿＿＿＿＿
8. 車庫 ＿＿＿＿＿＿＿＿＿

---

67 足

ソク
あし、た・りる、た・す
foot, leg, enough, add

足 represents the shape of the lower part of the *leg*, beneath the knee joint.

Example sentences and meaning

1. foot, leg

* 若い人は足が長い。
 Young people have long legs.

2. depart

* 高尾山に遠足に行く
 to go on an excursion to Mount Takao

3. be enough, sufficient

* 時間が足りない。
 There isn't enough time.

4. add

* 二足す三は五です。
 Two plus three equals five.

Common compounds

満足	まんぞく	satisfaction
不足	ふそく	shortage, lack of
蛇足	だそく	superfluous, redundant
三足	さんそく	three pairs of socks
自給自足	じきゅうじそく	self-sufficiency

足 ← somewhat smaller than bottom half

7 丶 口 口 무 무 무 足

足

68 赤

セキ、*シャク
あか、あか・い、
あか・らめる

red, redden

赤 used to be written 灻 which combined *big* 大 and *fire* 火. A big fire was, of course, *red.*

Example sentences and meaning

1. red

* 信号は赤だ。
  It's a red light.
* 赤ちゃんが泣いた。
  The baby cried.
* 赤いセーターを見せて下さい。
  Please show me the red sweater.

2. become red, blush

* 彼は顔を赤らめた。
  He blushed.

3. complete

* あの人は赤の他人です。
  That person is a complete stranger.

Common compounds

赤道	せきどう	equator
赤字	あかじ	in the red, deficit
赤飯	せきはん	rice cooked with red beans
赤外線	せきがいせん	infrared rays
*真っ赤	まっか	deep red, crimson

赤 ← stroke ends with hook

7 一 十 土 ナ 亓 赤 赤

69 花

カ
はな

flower

花 combines *plants* 艹 and *change* 化 to indicate the *flowering* of a plant.

Example sentences and meaning

1. flower

* お祝いに花を贈る
  to send flowers on a special occasion
* 春先は花粉症になる
  to suffer from hay fever in early spring

2. splendid and gorgeous

* 花火を見に行こう。
  Let's go watch the fireworks.
* 花嫁さんはきれいだなあ。
  The bride is so beautiful!

Common compounds

生け花	いけばな	ikebana
開花	かいか	bloom, blossom
花びら	はなびら	petal
花見	はなみ	cherry-blossom viewing
造花	ぞうか	artificial flower

end stroke firmly → 花 ← stroke ends with hook

7 一 艹 艹 艹 䒑 花 花

70 貝
かい
sea shell

貝 originally depicted a *bivalve*, although it presently looks more like an overhead view of a single *shell with feelers*.

Example sentences and meaning

1. shell, shellfish

* きれいな貝殻を拾った。
  I picked up some beautiful shells.
* 貝の刺身はあまり好きじゃない。
  I don't like raw shellfish very much.
* その話になると彼は貝のようにかたく口を閉ざした。
  When the subject came up, he clammed right up.

Common compounds

巻き貝	まきがい	spiral shell or conch
二枚貝	にまいがい	bivalve
赤貝	あかがい	ark shell
貝類	かいるい	shellfish

貝 ⇐ equal spacing

7 | 丨 冂 冂 月 冃 目 貝 貝

貝

71 学
ガク
まな・ぶ
learning, study

学 can be thought of as a *child* 子 under a *roof* 宀, to suggest *learning*.

Example sentences and meaning

1. to study, learn

* 少しドイツ語を学んだ。
  I learned a little German.
* 三年間スウェーデンに留学した。
  I went to Sweden to study for three years.

2. learning

* 医学博士の学位をとった。
  I received my doctorate in medicine.
* 数学は苦手だった。
  I was poor at mathematics.

3. school

* 大学で英語を勉強した。
  I studied English at university.

Common compounds

学校	がっこう	school
学生	がくせい	student
独学	どくがく	self-study
化学	かがく	chemistry
心理学	しんりがく	psychology

resembles katakana ツ → 学
← stroke ends with hook

8 | ⸍ ⸌ ツ ⺍ 兴 学 学 学

学

金

キン、コン
かね、*かな
money, gold

72

金 represents *treasures* ㅛ in the *ground* 土 with a *covering* ᐱ over them. The treasures are *gold*.

Example sentences and meaning

1. money

* 現金で払います。
I'll pay in cash.

2. gold

* 十八金とルビーの指輪を買った。
I bought an 18-carat gold and ruby ring.

3. metal

* 弟は金属アレルギーがある。
My younger brother is allergic to metal.

4. abbreviation of 金曜日 (Friday)

* 来週の水木金は休みます。
Next week I will take Wednesday, Thursday, and Friday off.

Common compounds

金髪	きんぱつ	blond hair
金庫	きんこ	safe, cashbox
料金	りょうきん	fee, charge, fare
金融	きんゆう	credit, financing
税金	ぜいきん	tax

→ 金 ← slanted strokes do not touch base

8 ノ 入 人 今 牟 余 余 金 金

金

Test 3

Test 3 (1-72)

A   Write in kanji and kana

1. shortage　　不＿＿＿
2. equator　　＿＿＿道
3. fireworks　　＿＿＿ ＿＿＿
4. spiral shell　　巻 ＿＿＿ ＿＿
5. admission into school　　＿＿＿ ＿＿＿
6. cash　　現＿＿＿
7. excursion　　遠＿＿＿
8. baby　　＿＿＿ ＿＿＿ ＿＿＿ ＿＿＿
9. ikebana　　＿＿＿ ＿＿＿ ＿＿＿
10. university　　＿＿＿ ＿＿＿
11. Friday　　＿＿＿曜＿＿＿
12. neutrality　　＿＿＿ ＿＿＿
13. 100 pairs (of socks)　　＿＿＿ ＿＿＿
14. 85 years　　＿＿ ＿＿ ＿＿ ＿＿
15. air　　空＿＿＿
16. full name　　氏＿＿＿
17. teacher, doctor　　＿＿＿ ＿＿＿
18. early shift　　＿＿＿番
19. summer holiday　　夏 ＿＿＿ ＿＿＿
20. crybaby　　泣 ＿＿＿ ＿＿＿

B. Write in hiragana and katakana

1. 満足　＿＿＿＿＿＿＿＿＿
2. 真っ赤　＿＿＿＿＿＿＿＿＿
3. 花嫁　＿＿＿＿＿＿＿＿＿
4. 赤貝　＿＿＿＿＿＿＿＿＿
5. 留学　＿＿＿＿＿＿＿＿＿
6. 料金　＿＿＿＿＿＿＿＿＿
7. 足が長い　＿＿＿＿＿＿＿＿＿
8. 赤外線　＿＿＿＿＿＿＿＿＿
9. 開花　＿＿＿＿＿＿＿＿＿
10. 貝の刺身　＿＿＿＿＿＿＿＿＿
11. 心理学　＿＿＿＿＿＿＿＿＿
12. 税金　＿＿＿＿＿＿＿＿＿
13. 毛糸　＿＿＿＿＿＿＿＿＿
14. 竹串　＿＿＿＿＿＿＿＿＿
15. 防虫剤　＿＿＿＿＿＿＿＿＿
16. パンの耳　＿＿＿＿＿＿＿＿＿
17. 見物　＿＿＿＿＿＿＿＿＿
18. 四丁目　＿＿＿＿＿＿＿＿＿
19. 水車　＿＿＿＿＿＿＿＿＿
20. 村長　＿＿＿＿＿＿＿＿＿

C. Write in kanji and kana

1. じなん　　次＿＿＿
2. たりない　　＿＿＿ ＿＿＿ ＿＿＿ ＿＿＿

3. あからめる　　＿＿＿ ＿＿＿ ＿＿＿
4. はなびら　　＿＿＿ ＿＿＿ ＿＿＿
5. にまいがい　　＿＿＿枚＿＿＿
6. がっこう　　＿＿＿校
7. ぜいきん　　税＿＿＿
8. りっしゅん　　＿＿＿春
9. やおや　　＿＿＿ ＿＿＿屋
10. きんねん　　近＿＿＿
11. てんき　　＿＿＿ ＿＿＿
12. みょうじ　　＿＿＿ ＿＿＿
13. せんげつ　　＿＿＿ ＿＿＿
14. はやかわ　　＿＿＿ ＿＿＿
15. きゅうじつ　　＿＿＿ ＿＿＿
16. せきじゅうじ　　＿＿＿ ＿＿＿ ＿＿＿
17. いとをひく　　＿＿＿ ＿＿＿引＿＿＿
18. たけのこ　　＿＿＿ ＿＿＿
19. ほんのむし　　＿＿＿ ＿＿＿
20. はつみみ　　初＿＿＿

D. Match the kanji with its reading

1. 花見　＿＿＿　　a. かふんしょう
2. 町会　＿＿＿　　b. きんぱつ
3. 下車　＿＿＿　　c. はなみ
4. 村上　＿＿＿　　d. たはた
5. 男優　＿＿＿　　e. はなび
6. 自給自足　＿＿＿　　f. だんゆう
7. 赤飯　＿＿＿　　g. がくせい
8. 花粉症　＿＿＿　　h. いきる
9. 貝類　＿＿＿　　i. じきゅうじそく
10. 留学　＿＿＿　　j. ほうせき
11. 金髪　＿＿＿　　k. げしゃ
12. 水不足　＿＿＿　　l. かいるい
13. 赤字　＿＿＿　　m. むらかみ
14. 花火　＿＿＿　　n. せきはん
15. 貝殻　＿＿＿　　o. ちょうかい
16. 学生　＿＿＿　　p. かいがら
17. 金属　＿＿＿　　q. りゅうがく
18. 生きる　＿＿＿　　r. みずぶそく
19. 宝石　＿＿＿　　s. きんぞく
20. 田畑　＿＿＿　　t. あかじ

E   Rewrite in Japanese and translate

1. ストッキング　にそく

＿＿＿＿＿＿＿＿＿＿＿＿＿＿＿＿

2. あかい　はな　を　ください。

＿＿＿＿＿＿＿＿＿＿＿＿＿＿＿＿

3. まきがい と あかがい を ひろった。

   _____

4. だいがく で スペインご を まなぶ

   _____

5. おかね を きんこ に いれる

   _____

6. さん たす なな は じゅう です。

   _____

7. かがく と すうがく の クラス を
   やすむ

   _____

8. その きんぱつ の じょせい は あか
   の たにん です。

   _____

9. あの ほんや で がくせい が ふたり
   たち よみ を している。

   _____

10. りっぱ な きんぞく で できた バッ
   ジ を ひゃっこ かいました。

   _____

73 空

クウ
そら、あ・く、あ・ける、
から
sky, emptiness

空 combines *hole* 穴 and *work upon* 工. This concept suggests a room, which encloses *space*. From this came the meaning of *sky* and *emptiness*.

Example sentences and meaning

1. sky

* 空がきれいだなあ。
The sky is so beautiful.
* 成田空港は遠い。
Narita Airport is far.

2. empty, vacant

* この席、空いてますか。
Is this seat free?

3. empty, clear

* 料理のための場所を空ける
to clear some room to do some cooking

4. futile, groundless

* それは机上の空論だよ。
That theory only looks good on paper!

Common compounds

空気	くうき	air, atmosphere
空白	くうはく	blank, empty space
星空	ほしぞら	starry sky
空車	くうしゃ	empty taxi
空手	からて	karate

end stroke firmly → 空 ← this stroke longer

8 丶 宀 宀 穴 空 空 空

空

74 青

セイ、ショウ
あお、あお・い
blue, green

青 depicted *plant life* 生 by a *well* 井, which was *green*. Some believe that *blue* comes from the color of the water in the well.

Example sentences and meaning

1. blue, green

* どうしたの、顔色が真っ青だよ。
What's the matter? You're very pale.
* 信号が青に変わった。
The traffic light changed to green.

2. youth, immature

* なに青くさいこと、言ってるの。
What an immature thing to say!
* 青春時代を思い出す
to remember one's younger days

Common compounds

青空	あおぞら	blue sky
青年	せいねん	youth
群青色	ぐんじょういろ	navy blue
青森	あおもり	Aomori (place)
青木	あおき	Aoki (name)

青 ← stroke ends with hook

8 一 十 キ 主 主 青 青 青

青

75 林

リン
はやし
woods, forest

林 combines two of the characters for *tree* 木, suggesting trees or bamboo growing together in a *woods*.

Example sentences and meaning

1. **woods, forest**

* 山の奥まで林道が通っている。
A forest road runs deep into the mountains.
* 林の中を散歩する
to go for a stroll through the woods

2. **grouping, place where things are gathered**

* 林立する新宿のビル
Shinjuku's towering buildings

Common compounds

森林	しんりん	woods, forest
林業	りんぎょう	forestry
松林	まつばやし	pine forest
密林	みつりん	dense forest, jungle
小林	こばやし	Kobayashi (name)

林 ← stroke tapers off

8 一 十 才 木 朮 村 村 林

林

76 雨

ウ
あめ、*あま、*さめ、*ゆ
rain

雨 combines three things: *heaven* 一, *clouds* 冂, and 丬 *rain falling*.

Example sentences and meaning

1. **rain**

* 急に雨が降ってきた。
It suddenly started to rain.
* 小雨なら傘は要らない。
I won't need an umbrella if it's just drizzling.
* あしたの天気予報は大雨だ。
Heavy rain is forecast for tomorrow.
* 梅雨の頃は蒸し暑い。
It's muggy during the rainy season.

Common compounds

風雨	ふうう	wind and rain
長雨	ながあめ	long spell of rainy weather
暴風雨	ぼうふうう	windy rainstorm
豪雨	ごうう	heavy rain, downpour
*雨漏り	あまもり	leak in the roof

stroke ends firmly → 雨 ← stroke ends with hook

8 一 冂 冂 币 雨 雨 雨 雨

雨

77 草　ソウ　くさ　grass

草 combines *plant* 艹 and *early* 早, a reference to *seedlings* and *small plants*.

Example sentences and meaning

1. grass, small plants

* 庭の草むしりがたいへんだ。
It's hard work weeding the garden.
* 料理に香草を少し入れる
to add a few herbs to one's cooking

2. crude, rough

* 僕は草野球チームに入っている。
I'm a member of an amateur baseball team.

3. beginning, commence

* コンピューターグラフィックスの草分け
a pioneer in computer graphics

4. rough copy

* スピーチの草稿を手直しする
to touch up the draft of one's speech

Common compounds

海草	かいそう	seaweed
雑草	ざっそう	weeds
草食	そうしょく	herbivorous
道草	みちくさ	loiter
*煙草	たばこ	tobacco, cigarette

草 ← this stroke longest

9　一 十 艹 艹 芌 芢 苩 苩 草 草

78 音　オン、イン　おと、ね　sound

音 is a derivation of 言 *speak*, with a line in 口 *mouth* to represent the tongue making a *sound*.

Example sentences and meaning

1. sound

* 留守番電話に録音する
to record on an answering machine

2. music, melody

* どんな音楽が好きですか。
What kind of music do you like?

3. speech, pronunciation

* 発音がいいですね。
You have good pronunciation.

4. news, communication

* 二年前から彼から何の音沙汰もない。
I haven't heard anything from him in two years.

Common compounds

雑音	ざつおん	noise, static
足音	あしおと	sound of footsteps
騒音	そうおん	noise
音声	おんせい	voice, audio
音読み	おんよみ	*on* (kanji) reading

equal spacing → → 音

9　丶 亠 立 立 产 产 音 音 音

79 校 コウ school

校 combines 木 *tree* and 交 *person sitting cross-legged,* and can be thought of as a place where people sit and study; i.e., a *school.*

Example sentences and meaning

1. **school**

* 行きたい高校に合格した。
   I was accepted into the high school I wanted to go to.

* 一年間予備校に通った。
   I attended a prep school for one year.

2. **examine and compare**

* 明日中に校正してください。
   Please proofread this by the end of tomorrow.

3. **military commander**

* 彼は海軍の将校になった。
   He became a naval officer.

Common compounds

学校	がっこう	school
初校	しょこう	first proofs
小学校	しょうがっこう	elementary school

校 ← end stroke firmly

10 一 十 オ オ オ ギ ギ 柿 柿 校

校

80 森 シン もり forest

森 consists of three 木 *tree* to give the idea of *forest.*

Example sentences and meaning

1. **woods, forest**

* 森林資源を守る
   to protect timber resources

* あの小さな森に行ってみよう。
   Let's go to that grove.

2. **silent, dignified state**

* 神社は森閑としていた。
   The shrine was very quiet.

Common compounds

森林	しんりん	woods, forest
森林開発	しんりんかいはつ	forest development
森田	もりた	Morita (name)
青森	あおもり	Aomori (place)

森 inner stroke of bottom left 木 is short

12 一 十 オ 木 杢 杢 촜 촜 森 森 森 森

森

Quiz 10

Quiz 10 (73-80)

A. Write in hiragana
1. 星空　　_____
2. 青春時代　_____
3. 小林　　_____
4. 小雨　　_____
5. 煙草　　_____
6. 発音　　_____
7. 高校　　_____
8. 森林開発　_____

B. Write in kanji
1. からて　　　　_____ _____
2. あおもり　　　_____ _____
3. まつばやし　　松_____
4. ながあめ　　　長_____
5. かいそう　　　海_____
6. あしおと　　　_____ _____
7. しょうがっこう　_____ _____ _____
8. もりた　　　　_____ _____
9. おんがく　　　_____楽
10. つゆ　　　　　梅_____

C. Write in kanji and kana
1. blank space　_____ _____
2. blue sky　　_____ _____
3. forest road　　　道
4. heavy rain　　_____ _____
5. weeding　　_____ _____ _____ _____
6. audio　　　　　声
7. proofreading　_____ _____
8. recording　　録_____

Review Test 1 (1–80)

A. Write in hiragana

1. 成田空港 _____
2. 真っ青 _____
3. 林業 _____
4. 梅雨 _____
5. 道草 _____
6. 音読み _____
7. 初校 _____
8. 森林資源 _____
9. 耳たぶ _____
10. 見方 _____
11. 町役場 _____
12. 車庫 _____
13. 農村 _____
14. 大男 _____
15. 早朝 _____
16. 年中無休 _____
17. 字典 _____
18. 糸偏 _____
19. 青竹 _____
20. 南京虫 _____

B. Write in English

1. 空車 _____
2. 青年 _____
3. 密林 _____
4. 豪雨 _____
5. 草分け _____
6. 録音 _____
7. 予備校 _____
8. 森林 _____
9. 両立 _____
10. 嘘八百 _____
11. 年賀状 _____
12. 気力 _____
13. 名産 _____
14. 優先 _____
15. 四季 _____
16. 右手 _____
17. 左折 _____
18. 玉乗り _____
19. 出前 _____
20. 正義 _____

C. Write in kanji

1. くうき ___ ___
2. あおき ___ ___

3. こばやし ___ ___
4. こさめ ___ ___
5. ざっそう 雑 ___
6. おんがく ___ 楽
7. がっこう ___ ___
8. なかもり ___ ___
9. すいようび ___ 曜 ___
10. ちゅうがくせい _____
11. がんじつ 元 ___
12. あまの ___ 野
13. さくぶん 作 ___
14. まつばやし 松 ___
15. さんぜんえん ___ ___ ___
16. じょおう ___ ___
17. かざん ___ ___
18. こんげつ 今 ___
19. こいぬ ___ ___
20. りょうて 両 ___

D. Write in kanji and kana

1. Haneda Airport 羽 ___ ___ 港
2. Aomori ___ ___
3. wind and rain 風 ___
4. herbivorous ___ 食
5. pronunciation 発 ___
6. prep school 予備 ___
7. forest development ___ 開発
8. underwear ___ 着
9. maximum, largest 最 ___
10. elementary school _____
11. emergency exit 非常 ___
12. Mount Fuji 富士 ___
13. prince ___ ___
14. popularity ___ 社
15. joining a company ___ 社
16. masterpiece ___ 作
17. March 3 ___ ___ ___
18. ¥1,000 note ___ ___ 札
19. improvement 向 ___
20. one week ___ 週間

E. Match the kanji with its reading

1. 二度 ___ a. じゅっぷん
2. 七日 ___ b. ぐんじょういろ
3. 八月八日 ___ c. にど
4. 九州生まれ ___ d. ほんまちどおり
5. 十分 ___ e. そうき

6.	空白	___	f. なのか
7.	群青色	___	g. もりぐち
8.	中林	___	h. ざつおん
9.	雨漏り	___	i. おとこのひと
10.	海草	___	j. くるまざ
11.	雑音	___	k. みみかき
12.	高校生	___	l. はちがつようか
13.	森口	___	m. なかばやし
14.	耳かき	___	n. くうはく
15.	見当	___	o. こうこうせい
16.	本町通り	___	p. むらはちぶ
17.	車座	___	q. きゅうしゅうう まれ
18.	村八分	___	r. けんとう
19.	男の人	___	s. かいそう
20.	早期	___	t. あまもり

F. Match the kanji with its English meaning

1.	十一月七日	___	a. potted plant
2.	暴力	___	b. village road
3.	千葉県	___	c. national university
4.	風下	___	d. full moon
5.	大小	___	e. November 7
6.	満月	___	f. evening newspaper
7.	握手	___	g. lawn
8.	花火	___	h. men and women
9.	男女	___	i. large and small
10.	夕刊	___	j. violence
11.	六ケ月	___	k. train, streetcar
12.	文章	___	l. facing left
13.	植木	___	m. deep red
14.	左向き	___	n. six months
15.	芝生	___	o. fireworks
16.	国立大学	___	p. downwind
17.	本日休業	___	q. writing
18.	真っ赤	___	r. closed today
19.	電車	___	s. Chiba Prefecture
20.	村道	___	t. shaking hands

G. Rewrite in Japanese and translate

1. あし の ながい おとこ の こ

    _____

2. むらかみさん の あかい くるま を みせて ください。

    _____

3. にほんじん は ほんとう に なまたまご を たべる の が すき です か。

    _____

4. さくじつ たなかくん は しんりんがく の ほん を て に いれた。

    _____

5. 1983ねん、じゅうがつ にじゅうよっか かようび に かわぐちせんせい は ゆうめい な ひゃっかじてん を しゅっぱん した。

    _____

6. たけださん は わかい のに しらが が あって、め が よく みえなく なって いる。

    _____

7. ちょきんばこ から ごひゃくえんだま を じゅうまい だして、みずたまもよう の ブラウス を かった。

    _____

8. むし が みみ の なか に はいって、くすぐったい。

    _____

9. どようび に つゆ が あけて、ひさしぶり に あおぞら が みえた。

    _____

10. かれ は あさ はやく がっこう へ いき、ゆうがた おそく かえります。

    _____

Second Grade Characters

List of Second Grade Characters

81. 刀	121. 光	161. 長	201. 強
82. 丸	122. 考	162. 直	202. 教
83. 弓	123. 行	163. 店	203. 黄
84. 工	124. 合	164. 東	204. 黒
85. 才	125. 寺	165. 歩	205. 細
86. 万	126. 自	166. 妹	206. 週
87. 引	127. 色	167. 明	207. 雪
88. 牛	128. 西	168. 門	208. 船
89. 元	129. 多	169. 夜	209. 組
90. 戸	130. 地	170. 科	210. 鳥
91. 午	131. 池	171. 海	211. 野
92. 公	132. 当	172. 活	212. 理
93. 今	133. 同	173. 計	213. 雲
94. 止	134. 肉	174. 後	214. 絵
95. 少	135. 米	175. 思	215. 間
96. 心	136. 毎	176. 室	216. 場
97. 切	137. 何	177. 首	217. 晴
98. 太	138. 角	178. 秋	218. 朝
99. 内	139. 汽	179. 春	219. 答
100. 父	140. 近	180. 食	220. 道
101. 分	141. 形	181. 星	221. 買
102. 方	142. 言	182. 前	222. 番
103. 毛	143. 谷	183. 茶	223. 園
104. 友	144. 作	184. 昼	224. 遠
105. 外	145. 社	185. 点	225. 楽
106. 兄	146. 図	186. 南	226. 新
107. 古	147. 声	187. 風	227. 数
108. 広	148. 走	188. 夏	228. 電
109. 市	149. 体	189. 家	229. 話
110. 矢	150. 弟	190. 記	230. 歌
111. 台	151. 売	191. 帰	231. 語
112. 冬	152. 麦	192. 原	232. 算
113. 半	153. 来	193. 高	233. 読
114. 母	154. 里	194. 紙	234. 聞
115. 北	155. 画	195. 時	235. 鳴
116. 用	156. 岩	196. 弱	236. 線
117. 羽	157. 京	197. 書	237. 親
118. 回	158. 国	198. 通	238. 頭
119. 会	159. 姉	199. 馬	239. 顔
120. 交	160. 知	200. 魚	240. 曜

81 刀

トウ
かたな
sword

刀 depicts a *sword* with a bent blade.

Example sentences and meaning

1. sword

* 小刀で鉛筆を削る
  to sharpen a pencil with a pocket knife
* 刀は武士の命と言われた。
  The sword was said to be the "life" of the samurai.
* 日本刀は美術品として価値がある。
  Japanese swords are valued as works of art.
* 記者は大統領に単刀直入に質問した。
  The journalists questioned the president in a direct manner.

Common compounds

木刀	ぼくとう	wooden sword
短刀	たんとう	short sword, dagger
*竹刀	しない	bamboo sword (used in kendō)

stroke does not → 刀
protrude

2 ﾌ 刀

刀

82 丸

ガン
まる、まる・い
circle, entire, round

丸 was originally written showing a *person huddled* メ at the base of a *cliff* 乁. From this came the meaning of *round*.

Example sentences and meaning

1. round

* 丸顔なので丸ちゃんと呼ばれています。
  She's called Maru-chan because of her round face.

2. complete, entire

* 丸暗記する
  to rote memorize
* 日本に来て丸一年になります。
  A whole year has passed since I came to Japan.

3. suffix used to name ships

* 日本丸という船
  a ship called Nippon-Maru

Common compounds

弾丸	だんがん	bullet
一丸	いちがん	a lump, rolled into one
丸太	まるた	log
丸ごと	まるごと	whole, entirely
丸薬	がんやく	pill

丸 ← stroke ends with hook

3 ﾉ 九丸

丸

83 弓

キュウ
ゆみ
bow

弓 derives from a pictograph of a *bow*.

Example sentences and meaning

1. bow

* 姉は弓道を習っている。
  My older sister is learning Japanese archery.

* バイオリンを弓で弾く
  to play a violin with a bow

Common compounds

弓矢	ゆみや	bow and arrow
洋弓	ようきゅう	Western archery
弓なり	ゆみなり	arch, curve
胡弓	こきゅう	Chinese fiddle
真弓	まゆみ	Mayumi (name)

弓 ← stroke ends with hook

3 | フ コ 弓

弓

84 工

コウ、ク
artisan, construction

工 depicts an ancient carpenter's *tool*, from which derived the meaning of *work*.

Example sentences and meaning

1. industry, artisan

* 竹の伝統工芸品に興味があります。
  I'm interested in traditional bamboo handicrafts.

* 自動車工場を見学する
  to visit an automobile factory

* 大工さんに家の改築を頼む
  to hire a carpenter to do house alterations

2. job, work

* その道は工事中で通れないよ。
  You can't get through because they're fixing the road.

Common compounds

工業	こうぎょう	industry
工程	こうてい	work progress, process
細工	さいく	workmanship, trick
木工	もっこう	woodworking, carpenter
工藤	くどう	Kudō (name)

工 ← this stroke longer than one above

3 | 一 丁 工

工

85 才 サイ
ability, years old

才 originally depicted a *dam in a river*. The character's present meanings resulted from phonetic borrowing.

Example sentences and meaning

1. **natural talent**

* この子は絵の才能がある。
  This child has a talent for drawing.

* モーツアルトは天才だった。
  Mozart was a genius.

2. **used instead of 歳 to indicate age**

* お酒は二十才になってから。
  The drinking age is 20.

Common compounds

才気	さいき	talent, resourcefulness
商才	しょうさい	business ability
青二才	あおにさい	inexperienced youth, novice
多才	たさい	many talents
才色兼備	さいしょくけんび	wit and beauty

才 ← protrudes slightly

3 一 十 才

才

86 万 マン、バン
*よろず
ten thousand, all sorts of

万 derived from a pictograph of a *scorpion*, pronounced *man* in Chinese. From phonetic borrowing and perhaps because scorpions were very numerous, the character became associated with *ten thousand*.

Example sentences and meaning

1. **ten thousand**

* サイクロンで十万人以上の死者が出た。
  The cyclone caused more than one hundred thousand deaths.

* 一万円下ろす
  to withdraw ten thousand yen

2. **countless, all**

* 万有引力の法則
  the law of universal gravitation

* 万が一にもそんなことはないと思うよ。
  There isn't a chance in a million that would ever happen.

Common compounds

万歳	ばんざい	Hurrah! Long live . . .
万葉集	まんようしゅう	*Manyōshū*
万年筆	まんねんひつ	fountain pen
万国博覧会	ばんこくはくらんかい	world's fair

万 ← stroke ends with hook

3 一 フ 万

万

Quiz 11 (81-86)

A. Write in kanji
1. にほんとう ___ ___ ___
2. まるた ___ 太
3. まゆみ 真 ___
4. こうじょう ___ 場
5. てんさい ___ ___
6. じゅうまんにん ___ ___
7. こがたな ___ ___
8. まるいちねん ___ ___ ___

B. Write in English
1. 弓道 _____
2. 大工 _____
3. 多才 _____
4. 万年筆 _____
5. 短刀 _____
6. 丸顔 _____
7. バイオリンの弓 _____
8. 細工 _____
9. 才能 _____
10. 十一万円 _____

C. Write in hiragana
1. 木刀 _____
2. 弾丸 _____
3. 弓矢 _____
4. 工芸品 _____
5. 青二才 _____
6. 万歳 _____
7. 竹刀 _____
8. 丸暗記 _____

---

87 引

イン
ひ・く、ひ・ける
pull, attract, close

引 combines *bow* 弓 and *string* ｜ to suggest *pulling*.

Example sentences and meaning

1. to pull, draw
* 戸を引いて下さい。
  Please pull open the door.
* 海の近くに引っ越す
  to move (to a house) near the sea

2. guide, extend
* グラウンドに白線を引く
  to draw white lines on a playing field

3. bring from elsewhere
* マクベスの台詞を引用する
  to quote lines from *Macbeth*

4. lower a number, price
* 二割引きでラジカセを買った。
  I bought a radio-cassette player at a 20 percent discount.

Common compounds

引力	いんりょく	gravitation
値引き	ねびき	discount
引き潮	ひきしお	ebb tide
強引	ごういん	by force, forcibly
取引	とりひき	business, transaction

引 ← end stroke firmly

4　フ　コ　弓　引

引

88 牛 ギュウ / うし / COW, OX

牛 derived from a pictograph of a *cow's head and horns*, viewed from the front.

Example sentences and meaning

1. cow, ox

* 毎日牛乳を飲む
to drink milk every day

* 牛肉があるので、今夜はすきやきにしよう。
Since we have some beef, let's eat sukiyaki tonight.

* このバッグは牛革ですか。
Is this handbag leather?

* 今でも牛を使って畑仕事をする所がある。
Even now there are still places where oxen are used for farm work.

Common compounds

闘牛	とうぎゅう	bullfight
水牛	すいぎゅう	water buffalo
野牛	やぎゅう	bison, buffalo
乳牛	にゅうぎゅう	dairy cow

this stroke longer → 牛 ← stroke protrudes
than one above

4 ノ ⊢ ⊢ 牛

牛

89 元 ゲン、ガン / もと / source, root, origin

元 derived from a pictograph of a person's *head and neck*, symbolizing *origin* and *source*.

Example sentences and meaning

1. origin, beginning

* どうしたの？元気がないね。
What's the matter? You look depressed.

* ガスの元栓を締める
to close a gas valve

2. formerly

* 使ったら元のところに返して下さい。
If you use it, please return it to where it was.

* 元首相が来日しました。
The former prime minister came to Japan.

3. first year in an era

* 私たちは平成元年に結婚した。
We got married in the first year of the Heisei era.

Common compounds

元素	げんそ	element (chemical)
根元	ねもと	root, base
地元	じもと	local
中元	ちゅうげん	summer gift-giving
元手	もとで	capital, funds

this stroke longer than → 元 ← stroke ends with hook
than the one above it

4 一 二 テ 元

元

90 戸

コ
と、*べ

door, household

戸 derived from a pictograph of one half of a *double door* or *gate*.

Example sentences and meaning

1. **door**
   * その戸は押して下さい。
     Please push that door open.

2. **counter for houses, house**
   * 一戸建ての家に住みたいなあ。
     I'd like to live in my own house.
   * 役所に戸籍謄本を取りにいく
     to go to a government office to get a copy of the family register

Common compounds

戸外	こがい	outdoor, open-air
引き戸	ひきど	sliding door
網戸	あみど	screen door
雨戸	あまど	shutter, storm door
*神戸	こうべ	Kōbe (place)

stroke tapers off → 戸

4 一 ラ ラ 戸

戸

91 午

ゴ

noon

午 originated from a pictograph of a *wooden pestle*. It came to have the meaning of *noon,* the middle of the day, perhaps because a pestle hits the middle of a mortar.

Example sentences and meaning

1. **noon, midday**
   * 午前中にこの仕事をやっておいて下さい。
     Please attend to this business this morning.
   * 午後なら行けます。
     I'll be able to go in the afternoon.

2. **south**
   * 子午線は北極と南極を結ぶ線です。
     A meridian is a line that links the North and South Poles.

Common compounds

午前	ごぜん	morning, A.M.
午後	ごご	afternoon, P.M.
正午	しょうご	noon
午餐	ごさん	luncheon
端午の節句	たんごのせっく	Children's Day (May 5)

午 ← this stroke longer than one above

4 ノ 二 午

午

92 公

コウ
おおやけ
public

公 derived from the *breaking up* 八 of *private property* ム; i.e., making it *public* property.

Example sentences and meaning

1. government, public office

* 父は公務員でした。
My father was a government official.

2. society, community

* 70年代から公害がひどくなってきた。
Pollution has worsened since the 1970s.

3. unconcealed, in the open

* 事件が公になった。
That case was made public.

4. unprejudiced

* 公平な裁判
a fair trial

Common compounds

公共	こうきょう	public society, community
公募	こうぼ	public appeal
公認	こうにん	officially authorized, certified
公言	こうげん	declaration

stroke bends sharply → 公 ← leave gap

| 4 | ノ | 八 | 公 | 公 | | | |

公

Quiz 12 (87-92)

A. Write in hiragana and katakana

1. 引き潮 _____
2. 牛乳 _____
3. ガスの元栓 _____
4. 神戸 _____
5. 午後 _____
6. 公害 _____
7. 値引き _____
8. 水牛 _____

B. Write in kanji

1. もとしゅしょう　____首相
2. あまど　____ ____
3. ごぜんちゅう　____ ____ ____
4. こうへい　____平
5. ごういん　強____
6. ぎゅうにく　____肉
7. げんき　____ ____
8. こがい　____外
9. しょうご　____午
10. こうむいん　____務員

C. Write in kanji

1. gravitation ____ ____
2. dairy cow 乳____
3. the first year of the Heisei era 平成____ ____
4. screen door 網____
5. A.M. ____前
6. declaration ____言
7. discount 値____ ____
8. buffalo 野____

93 今　キン、コン　いま

now, this, immediately

今 depicts something being *covered* to prevent its escape. The meaning of *now* and *immediately* perhaps came from covering it *quickly*.

Example sentences and meaning

1. now

* 今電話中です。
  He is on the phone at the moment.
* たった今帰りました。
  He just left to go home.

2. this

* 今週の予定を立てる
  to make this week's schedule
* 今朝は寒い。
  It is cold this morning.

3. immediately

* ただ今参ります。
  He is coming soon.

Common compounds

今週	こんしゅう	this week
今日	きょう	today
今月	こんげつ	this month
今度	こんど	next time

strokes taper off → 今 ←

4 　ノ　∧　∧　今

今

94 止　シ　と・まる

stop

止 originally depicted the *foot* and *toes*, from which later came the meaning of *stop*.

Example sentences and meaning

1. stop moving

* 時計が止まっている。
  My watch has stopped.

2. cease, stop (an action)

* あれは駐車禁止の標識です。
  That's a No Parking sign.
* 雨で試合が中止になった。
  The match was called off because of rain.
* なかなか煙草が止められない。
  I just can't manage to quit smoking.

Common compounds

休止	きゅうし	pause, suspension
止血	しけつ	stop bleeding
防止	ぼうし	prevention
行き止まり	いきどまり	dead end, impasse

stroke extends → 止

4 　｜　⊦　⊦　止

止

95 少

ショウ
すく・ない、すこ・し
little, few

少 combines *small* 小 with an added stroke representing a *sword*. Thus it is a small object being made even *smaller*.

Example sentences and meaning

1. **little, few**
* 頭が少し痛い。
I have a slight headache.
* 少々お待ち下さい。
Please wait a moment.

2. **young, junior**
* 少年少女向きの本を書いています。
I am writing a book aimed at young boys and girls.
* これは幼少の頃の写真です。
This is a photograph of me as a child.

Common compounds

最少	さいしょう	fewest, youngest
少額	しょうがく	small amount
減少	げんしょう	decrease, reduction
少量	しょうりょう	small amount

ends with hook → 少 ← end stroke firmly center stroke

4 丨 丿 小 少

少

96 心

シン
こころ
heart, mind

心 depicts the shape of the *heart*.

Example sentences and meaning

1. **heart**
* ジョギング中に心臓の発作を起こした。
He had a heart attack while jogging.

2. **mind, spirit**
* ご親切に心からお礼申し上げます。
I offer you my heartfelt gratitude for your kindness.
* 大丈夫だからもう心配しないで。
Don't worry—everything will be all right.
* 大学で心理学を勉強した。
I studied psychology at university.

3. **center, vital place**
* 問題の核心を突く質問をする
to ask a question that gets to the heart of the matter

Common compounds

中心	ちゅうしん	center
安心	あんしん	feel relieved, peace of mind
熱心	ねっしん	enthusiasm
感心	かんしん	be impressed by, admire
重心	じゅうしん	center of gravity

end stroke firmly → 心 ← stroke ends with hook

4 丶 心 心 心

心

97 切

セツ、*サイ
き・る、き・れる
cut, sharp

切 combines *sword* 刀 and the act of *cutting in two* ᄂ, emphasizing the meaning of *cut*.

Example sentences and meaning

1. **cut with a tool**
   * 髪を切ろうと思います。
   I think I'll have my hair cut.

2. **interrupt, be interrupted**
   * 突然電話が切れた。
   Suddenly the telephone went dead.

3. **limit, cut off**
   * 本棚で部屋を二つに仕切る。
   to divide the room in two with a bookcase

4. **run out of, used up**
   * 売り切れです。
   We're sold out.

Common compounds

切断	せつだん	cutting, amputation
親切	しんせつ	kind, friendly
大切	たいせつ	important
期限切れ	きげんぎれ	overdue, expired
*一切	いっさい	entirely, all, everything

切 ← stroke ends with hook

4 ᄂ t 切 切

切

98 太

タイ、タ
ふと・い、ふと・る
fat, thick, gain weight

太 originally combined *big* 大 and *two* 二, emphasizing the idea of something *very large*. 二 was later simplified to one dot.

Example sentences and meaning

1. **width, girth, get fat**
   * 最近少し太った。
   I've put on a little weight lately.
   * もう少し太い糸がありますか。
   Do you have a slightly thicker thread?

2. **large**
   * 太陽が眩しい。
   The sun is dazzling.

3. **highly exalted**
   * 皇太子殿下
   His Highness the Crown Prince

Common compounds

太鼓	たいこ	drum
丸太	まるた	log
太もも	ふともも	thigh
太刀	たち	sword
太平洋	たいへいよう	Pacific Ocean

太 don't mistake for 犬

4 一 ナ 大 太

太

Quiz 13 (93-98)

A. Write in English
1. 今朝 _____
2. 駐車禁止 _____
3. 少年少女 _____
4. 心配 _____
5. 大切 _____
6. 皇太子 _____
7. 中心 _____
8. 防止 _____

B. Match the kanji with its reading
1. 少し _____ a. いきどまり
2. 安心 _____ b. ちゅうしん
3. 切断 _____ c. あんしん
4. 太平洋 _____ d. こんしゅう
5. 今週 _____ e. すこし
6. 行き止まり _____ f. たいへいよう
7. 少々 _____ g. たいよう
8. 中心 _____ h. せつだん
9. 売り切れ _____ i. しょうしょう
10. 太陽 _____ j. うりきれ

C. Write in kanji and kana
1. こんげつ ___ ___
2. ちゅうし ___ ___
3. すくない ___ ___ ___
4. しんりがく ___理___
5. しんせつ 親___
6. ふともも ___ ___ ___
7. きょう ___ ___
8. やめられない ___ ___ ___ ___
   ___

---

99 内 ナイ、*ダイ
うち
inside, within

内 combines *enclosure* 冂 and *go in* 入 to give the idea of *inside*.

Example sentences and meaning

1. within an area, boundary
* それは国内(こくない)では売(う)っていません。
  It isn't sold domestically.
* 仕事(しごと)の内容(ないよう)を教(おし)えて下(くだ)さい。
  Please tell me about the job.
* 博物館(はくぶつかん)の案内図(あんないず)をもらう
  to receive a map of the museum

2. within a certain period
* 話(はなし)は三分以内(さんぷんいない)にして下(くだ)さい。
  Please say it within three minutes.

3. not open, secret, temporary
* トラブルを内密(ないみつ)に処理(しょり)する
  to deal with a problem secretly

Common compounds

内科	ないか	internal medicine
内閣	ないかく	the Cabinet
内心	ないしん	one's heart, mind
家内	かない	my wife, family
内田	うちだ	Uchida (name)

stroke protrudes → 内 ← stroke ends with hook

4 丨 冂 内 内

内

100 父

フ
ちち
father

父 derived from a pictograph of a *hand holding a stick*, which represented someone with power, i.e., a *father*.

Example sentences and meaning

1. father

* 父は若い頃テニスの選手だった。
  When he was young, my father was a tennis player.

* お父さん、このふた開けて。
  Dad, open this lid, will you?

* これは祖父の形見です。
  This is a keepsake from my grandfather.

2. uncle

* こちらは叔父です
  This is my uncle.

Common compounds

父母	ふぼ	mother and father
神父	しんぷ	priest, father
義父	ぎふ	father-in-law, stepfather
父方	ちちかた	on the father's side
祖父	そふ	grandfather

strokes taper off → 父 ←

4 　ノ　ハ　グ　父

父

101 分

ブン、フン、ブ
わ・ける、わ・かる
portion, minute, rate, divide, understand

分 combines 八 *cut in two* and 刀 *sword* to give the meaning of *divide*.

Example sentences and meaning

1. divided

* ケーキをみんなに分ける
  to divide the cake for everyone

2. minute

* 七時四十五分に予約がある。
  I have an appointment at 7:45.

3. identity, social standing

* 何か身分を証明するものを持っていますか。
  Do you have any ID?

4. state of affairs, extent

* 今日は気分がいいなあ。
  I feel fine today!

Common compounds

部分	ぶぶん	part
分解	ぶんかい	analysis, breakdown
自分	じぶん	oneself, one's own
草分け	くさわけ	pioneer, settler
十分	じゅうぶん／じっぷん	enough/ten minutes

leave space at top → 分 ← stroke ends with hook

4 　ノ　ハ　分　分

分

102 方

ホウ
かた
direction, person, way of (doing)

方 possibly derived from a pictograph of a *tethered boat,* floating in the *direction* of the current.

Example sentences and meaning

1. direction, way

* 池袋方面行きの電車が参ります。
  The train approaching is bound for Ikebukuro.

2. method, reason

* 早く予約した方がいいよ。
  You should make a reservation soon.

3. region, respective places

* その地方の方言はよく知らない。
  I don't know much about that region's dialect.

4. polite way to refer to someone

* 森田さんという方からお電話です。
  There is a telephone call from Mr. Morita.

Common compounds

両方	りょうほう	both
方法	ほうほう	method, means
読み方	よみかた	pronunciation of a character
夕方	ゆうがた	evening
味方	みかた	friend, ally

方 ← stroke bends

4 `ヽ 亠 方 方`

方

103 毛

モウ
け
hair

毛 represents an animal's *furry* tail held upright.

Example sentences and meaning

1. hair, fur

* このセーターは毛百パーセントですか。
  Is this sweater pure wool?
* 肩に髪の毛が付いているよ。
  There's a hair on your shoulder.
* 毛皮のコートは人気が下がっている。
  Fur coats are losing popularity.

2. growing of vegetation

* その地域は不毛の地だ。
  That region is a barren wasteland.

Common compounds

毛虫	けむし	caterpillar
眉毛	まゆげ	eyebrows
二毛作	にもうさく	two crops a year
直毛	ちょくもう	straight hair
毛深い	けぶかい	hairy

don't mistake for 手　毛 ← stroke ends with hook

4 `ノ 二 三 毛`

毛

| 104 友 | ユウ
とも
friend | 友 depicts *two hands,* a symbol of *friendship.* |

Example sentences and meaning

1. friend

* 友だちが京都に住んでいます。
  A friend of mine lives in Kyōto

* 今私には親友がいない。
  I don't have any close friends now.

2. be on good terms with, intimate

* 日本とその国は最近友好条約を結んだ。
  Japan has recently concluded a treaty of friendship with that country.

Common compounds

友人	ゆうじん	friend
友情	ゆうじょう	friendship, fellowship
級友	きゅうゆう	classmate
悪友	あくゆう	bad company/companions

| stroke protrudes → 友 |
| 4 一 ナ 方 友 |
| 友 | | | | | | |

Test 4 (81-104)

A. Write in hiragana
1. 国内 _____
2. お父さん _____
3. 気分 _____
4. 方言 _____
5. 毛虫 _____
6. 友だち _____
7. 日本刀 _____
8. 日本丸 _____
9. 洋弓 _____
10. 工事中 _____

B. Write in kanji and kana
1. うちだ _____ _____
2. しんぷ 神____
3. じぶん 自____
4. ちほう 地____
5. ゆうこう ____好
6. やぎゅう 野____
7. ごじゅうにさい ____ ____ ____ ____
8. まんがいち ____ ____ ____
9. とりひき 取____
10. ゆうじん ____ ____

C. Write in kanji
1. within three minutes ____ ____ 以 ____
2. on the father's side ____ ____
3. enough ____ ____
4. both 両____
5. straight hair 直____
6. friendship ____情
7. summer gift-giving ____ ____
8. Kōbe 神____
9. in the morning ____前 ____
10. fairness ____平

D. Write in English
1. 案内図を見る

_____

2. 叔父から一万円をもらった。

_____

3. 単刀直入に質問する

_____

4. その牛の目は丸くて大きい。

_____

5. 真弓さんは今日引っ越しです。

_____

6. 強引に戸をあける

_____

7. 元のところに車を止めなさい。

_____

8. 話を公にする

_____

9. 今父は太いふでで字を書いている。

_____

10. 少ない食べ物を分ける

_____

E. Fill in the kanji and translate
1. わたしの（とも だち）が（しんりがく 理 ）をべんきょうしている。
2. （くどう 藤 ）さんに（て 紙 ）を（だ ）そうとおもっていたが、（きって ）が（た ）りなかった。
3. （もうり 利 ）さんは（よんじゅっさい ）になって、（すこ ）し（ふと ）りはじめました。
4. （はくせん 線 ）の（うちがわ 側 ）をあるいて（くだ ）さい。
5. （うし ）は（うちやま ）さんの（ほう ）へはしっていった。
6. （ちち ）が（ばんゆういんりょく 有 ）のほうそくについてはなしてくれた。
7. この（でんしゃ 電 ）は（かわぐちほう めんゆき）ですか。
8. （きょう ）の（ごご 後）（ゆうじん ）が（たまち ）からくる。
9. （こうえん 園 ）の（すいどう 道 ）の（みず ）が（と ）まっていたので、ばいてんで（ぎゅうにゅう 乳 ）をかった。
10. （おとこ ）たちは（おお きな（まるた ）を（ひ ）いて、（もり ）の（なか ）から（で ）てきた。

105 外

ガイ、ゲ
そと、ほか、はず・す
external, other, remove

外 shows a *moon* 夕 and a *turtle shell* 卜, two objects that suggest *outside* and *external*.

Example sentences and meaning

1. outside, beyond a certain boundary

* 家の外に洗濯物を干す
  to dry the wash outside the house
* 外国へ行ったことがありません。
  I've never been abroad.

2. exterior, appear

* 人を外見だけで判断する
  to judge a person by his appearance

3. come off, remove, be away from

* 今席を外しております。
  He isn't at his desk at the moment.

4. something different, extra issue

* 号外が出た。
  They put out an extra edition.

Common compounds

外出	がいしゅつ	go out
意外	いがい	unexpected, surprising
内外	ないがい	inside and outside, domestic and foreign
外務省	がいむしょう	Ministry of Foreign Affairs

stroke tapers off → 外

5 ノ ク タ 夘 外

外

106 兄

ケイ、*キョウ
あに
elder brother

兄 combines *person* 儿 and *mouth* 口, suggesting an *elder brother* who advises his younger siblings.

Example sentences and meaning

1. elder brother

* ご兄弟がいらっしゃいますか。
  Do you have any brothers or sisters?
* 兄が二人います。
  I have two older brothers.
* お兄ちゃん、遊ぼうよ。
  Come on, let's play! (said to an older brother)

Common compounds

父兄	ふけい	parents and brothers, guardians
長兄	ちょうけい	eldest brother
次兄	じけい	one's second elder brother

兄 ← stroke ends with hook

5 丶 ロ ロ ア 兄

兄

107 古 コ
ふる・い、ふる・す
old, wear out

古 derived from a pictograph of a human skull, an object that represents something *old*.

Examples sentences and meaning

1. old

* 古い洋服を誰かにあげたい。
I'd like to give my old clothes to someone.

* きのう神田の古本屋に行った。
I went to a used bookstore in Kanda yesterday.

* 古典を読む
to read the classics

2. from ancient time

* 大学で考古学を専攻する
to major in archaeology at university

Common compounds

古風	こふう	old style, old custom
古寺	こじ	old temple
懐古	かいこ	nostalgia
稽古	けいこ	practice, rehearsal, workout
古川	ふるかわ	Furukawa (name)

古 ← this stroke longer than ones below it

5 一 十 十 古 古

古

108 広 コウ
ひろ・い、ひろ・まる、
ひろ・がる
broad, wide, spread, extend

広 combines *roof* 广 and *large* ム to indicate a *spacious* building.

Example sentences and meaning

1. wide, extend

* もっと広い家に住みたいなあ。
I'd love to live in a more spacious house!

* 目の前に真っ青な海が広がる。
The deep blue sea stretches out before me.

2. extend, spread, broaden

* 新聞の求人広告
a Help Wanted ad in a newspaper

* 噂はすぐ広まった。
The rumor spread in no time.

Common compounds

広場	ひろば	public square, plaza
広間	ひろま	hall, spacious room
背広	せびろ	business suit
広報	こうほう	publicity
広島	ひろしま	Hiroshima (place)

stroke tapers off → 広 ← make stroke connect

5 丶 亠 广 広 広

広

109 市

シ
いち

city, market

市 originally combined *stop* 止 and *balance* 平, indicating a place where people *stop* and *negotiate* goods.

Example sentences and meaning

1. market

* 毎日朝市が立つ。
  A morning market is held every day.
* 陶器市でいい茶碗を買った。
  I bought some nice rice bowls at the pottery fair.

2. bustling place

* 都市に人口が集中する。
  The population is concentrated in the cities.

3. city

* 市民センターで生け花教室が始まります。
  Flower arrangement classes will begin at the civic center.

Common compounds

市況	しきょう	market conditions
市長	しちょう	mayor
市役所	しやくしょ	city hall
株式市場	かぶしきしじょう	stock exchange

市 stroke ends with ← hook

5 　丶 亠 广 市 市

市

110 矢

シ
や

arrow

矢 derived from a pictograph of an *arrow* with a broad tip.

Example sentences and meaning

1. arrow

* 矢で的を射る
  to shoot an arrow at a target
* その部族は吹き矢で狩りをする。
  That tribe hunts with blowpipes.
* 月日は矢のように過ぎ去る。
  Time seems to slip through our fingers.

Common compounds

弓矢	ゆみや	bow and arrow
一矢	いっし	shoot back, retaliate
鏑矢	かぶらや	arrow with turnip-shaped head that whistles as it flies
矢印	やじるし	arrow, indicator

stroke does not protrude 矢 don't mistake for 失

5 ノ 一 乍 午 矢

矢

Quiz 14 (105-110)

A. Write in hiragana

1. 外務省 _____
2. ご兄弟 _____
3. 古本屋 _____
4. 広島 _____
5. 市役所 _____
6. 矢印 _____
7. 席を外す _____
8. 長兄 _____

C. Write in English

1. 外見 _____
2. 父兄 _____
3. 古典・ _____
4. 求人広告 _____
5. 株式市場 _____
6. 一矢 _____
7. 外出 _____
8. 次兄 _____

B. Write in kanji and kana

1. Furukawa
2. public square ＿＿＿場
3. morning market 朝＿＿
4. bow and arrow ＿＿＿＿
5. foreign country ＿＿国
6. older brother ＿＿＿ ＿ ＿
7. old temple ＿＿寺
8. business suit 背＿＿
9. mayor ＿＿長
10. blowpipe 吹＿＿ ＿

111

台

ダイ、タイ

stand, base

台 combines *self* ム and *mouth* 口 and in Chinese meant *name oneself*. The Japanese borrowed the character and used it to mean *stand, base*.

Example sentences and meaning

1. high, flat area

＊私の家は高台にあります。
My house stands on a bluff.

2. counter for vehicles, machines

＊車が一台家の前に止まった。
A car stopped in front of my house.

＊夜行寝台車で九州まで行った。
I went to Kyūshū on the overnight sleeper.

3. basis, base

＊この映画の台本がいいね。
This movie has a good story.

4. indicating a general range

＊ドルは百三十円台で推移している。
The dollar is shifting in the ¥130 range.

Common compounds

台所	だいどころ	kitchen
灯台	とうだい	lighthouse
舞台	ぶたい	stage
天文台	てんもんだい	observatory
台湾	たいわん	Taiwan

one stroke → 台

5 ｜ ㇗ ㇛ ㇟ 台 台

台

---

112 冬 トウ / ふゆ / winter

冬 derived from a pictograph of *two bags hanging from a rope* with the two dots in the middle representing ice, indicating that it was *winter*.

Example sentences and meaning

1. **winter**
   * 熊は冬眠する動物です。
     Bears are hibernating animals.
   * 次の冬季オリンピックはどこで開催されますか。
     Where will the next Winter Olympics be held?
   * 冬山登山は経験が要る。
     Mountain climbing in winter requires experience.
   * 冬物をバーゲンで買う
     to buy winter clothing at a sale

Common compounds

立冬	りっとう	the first day of winter
初冬	しょとう	beginning of winter
越冬	えっとう	pass the winter
冬休み	ふゆやすみ	winter vacation
冬至	とうじ	winter solstice

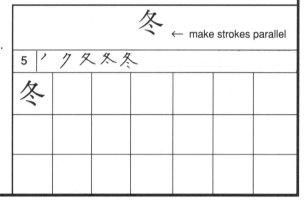
冬 ← make strokes parallel
5 ノ ク 冬 冬 冬

---

113 半 ハン / なか・ば / half

半 depicts a *cow* 牛 being *split* ` ´ in *half*.

Example sentences and meaning

1. **half**
   * ケーキを半分に切る
     to cut a cake in half
   * 番組の前半を見なかった。
     I missed the first half of the program.

2. **center, half past**
   * 七月の半ばに友だちが来る。
     A friend is coming around the middle of July.
   * 六時半に学校で会おう。
     Let's meet at the school at 6:30.

3. **midway, not complete**
   * このリボン、中途半端な長さだなあ。
     This ribbon is such an awkward length.

Common compounds

半月	はんげつ	half moon, semicircle
半島	はんとう	peninsula
大半	たいはん	majority, greater part
後半	こうはん	latter half
半人前	はんにんまえ	half portion

strokes slant in → 半 ← this stroke longer than one above it

5 丶 ソ ツ 兰 半
半

114 母

ボ、*モ
はは
mother

母 derived from a pictograph of a *seated woman*. The two dots represent the breasts.

Example sentences and meaning

1. mother

* 母は五年前に亡くなりました。
  My mother died five years ago.
* お母さん、私のお弁当はどこ？
  Mom, where's my box lunch?
* 母国語は絶対忘れないそうです。
  They say that you can't possibly forget your mother tongue.

2. aunt, wet nurse

* 保母さんになりたいと思います。
  I'd like to become a nursery school teacher.
* 叔母にお茶を習っています。
  I'm learning the tea ceremony from my aunt.

Common compounds

父母	ふぼ	mother and father
母乳	ぼにゅう	mother's milk
母国	ぼこく	one's native country
母校	ぼこう	one's alma mater
酵母	こうぼ	yeast

母 ← stroke ends with hook

5 く刀刀母母

母

115 北

ホク
きた
north

北 depicts *two people sitting back-to-back*, a reference to turning one's back and fleeing to the *north*.

Example sentences and meaning

1. north

* 北半球と南半球では季節が反対です。
  Seasons in the northern and southern hemispheres are reversed.
* まっすぐ北上すればその町に着きますよ。
  If you go directly north, you'll reach that town.

2. escape, be defeated

* 選挙ではじめて敗北した。
  He suffered his first defeat in the election.

Common compounds

北向き	きたむき	facing north
北極	ほっきょく	North Pole
北極星	ほっきょくせい	North Star
北海道	ほっかいどう	Hokkaidō (place)
*北京	ペキン	Beijing (place)

stroke goes up from left to the right → 北

5 一 十 寸 北 北

北

116 用

ヨウ
もち・いる
business, errand, use

用 depicts a *fence,* something *useful* to have.

Example sentences and meaning

1. employ, use

* 今、会議室は使用中です。
The conference room is presently in use.

* 急いで用意しなさい。
Hurry up and get ready!

2. function, useful

* この薬の作用によって風邪が治った。
This medicine cured my cold.

3. errand, work

* ちょっと用事があるので遅れます。
I have some work to do so I'll be late.

4. money, goods necessary for something

* 費用はどれぐらいかかりますか。
What will it cost?

Common compounds

用件	ようけん	an important matter
利用	りよう	use, make use of
急用	きゅうよう	urgent business
専用	せんよう	personal use, exclusively for
用紙	ようし	a form, stationery

stroke tapers off → 用 ← stroke ends with hook

5 丿 冂 月 月 用

用

Quiz 15 (111-116)

A. Write in kanji and kana

1. だいどころ ___ 所
2. ふゆやすみ ___ ___ ___
3. はんぶん ___ ___
4. ぼこくご ___ 国語
5. ほっかいどう ___ 海道
6. しようちゅう 使 ___ ___
7. てんもんだい ___ ___ ___
8. とうみん ___ 眠

B. Write in hiragana

1. 半島 _____
2. 母乳 _____
3. 北向き _____
4. 急用 _____
5. 夜行寝台車 _____
6. 冬山登山 _____
7. 半ば _____
8. お母さん _____
9. 北京 _____
10. 費用 _____

C. Write in English

1. 灯台 _____
2. 初冬 _____
3. 半人前 _____
4. 母校 _____
5. 北極 _____
6. 利用 _____
7. 台湾 _____
8. 越冬 _____

117 羽

ウ
はね、は
feather, wing

羽 represents long feathers of a bird's *wing*.

Example sentences and meaning

1. wing

* あのあひるは羽をけがしている。
That duck has hurt its wing.

2. feather

* 羽毛布団は軽くて暖かい。
Down comforters are light and warm.

3. counter for birds, rabbits

* 家でインコを二羽飼っています。
We have two parakeets at home.

Common compounds

羽音	はおと	sound of flapping wings
羽化	うか	grow wings
羽目	はめ	situation, predicament
羽田空港	はねだくうこう	Haneda Airport

羽　← strokes end with hook

6　フ　フ　习　羽　羽　羽

羽

118 回

カイ、*エ
まわ・る
times, go around

回 derived from a pictograph of a whirl to suggest *going around*.

Example sentences and meaning

1. go round, turn

* ＣＤが回らないよ。
The CD isn't spinning.

2. return, bring back

* プラスチック容器を回収する
to collect plastic containers (for recycling)

3. avoid

* 工事中なので迂回して下さい。
There is construction work going on, so please take the detour.

4. frequency

* もう一回言って下さい。
Could you say that again?

Common compounds

回覧	かいらん	circulate, read and pass on
回想	かいそう	reminisce, reflect on
今回	こんかい	this time, lately
次回	じかい	next time
回り道	まわりみち	roundabout way

回　greater in height than in width

6　｜　冂　冂　冋　回　回

回

119 会

カイ、エ

あ・う

society, understanding, meet

会 combines *lid* 𠆢 and pot of *rice* 云, which possibly meant *put together*, and then *come together*.

Example sentences and meaning

1. **meet a person**

* 友だちと会う約束がある。

I'm planning to meet a friend.

2. **gather, collect**

* 新人の歓迎会

a welcoming party for new employees

* 今課長は会議中です。

The section head is in a meeting now.

3. **turn out as one desires**

* 技術を会得する

to master a technique

4. **a particular time, occasion**

* 機会があったら、また会いましょう。

When we get the chance, let's get together again.

Common compounds

会計	かいけい	accounting, the bill
大会	たいかい	large meeting, tournament
会社	かいしゃ	company, corporation
教会	きょうかい	church
社会	しゃかい	society, social

会 ← this stroke longer than one above it

6　ノ　人　𠆢　会　会　会

---

120 交

コウ

まじ・る、か・わす

associate with, mix, exchange (greetings)

交 depicts a person sitting with *crossed legs*, which took on the meaning of *mix* and *exchange*.

Example sentences and meaning

1. **mix, associate with**

* 二年間交際して結婚しました。

They dated for two years before marrying.

* 社交ダンスをちょっと習いました。

I took ballroom dancing for a short while.

2. **be involved, intermixed**

* 交通事故が多い。

There are many traffic accidents.

3. **reciprocate, exchange greetings**

* おたがいに十分意見を交わした。

We exchanged views at length.

4. **alternately, substitute**

* 私たちは交替で料理を作っています。

We take turns at doing the cooking.

Common compounds

交友	こうゆう	friend, companion
国交	こっこう	diplomatic relations
交番	こうばん	police box
交差	こうさ	cross, intersect

stroke joins → 交 ← end stroke firmly

6　亠　亠　广　六　亦　交

交

121

光

コウ
ひかり、ひか・る

light, shine

光 shows a *person* 儿 carrying a *torch* 丷 giving off *light*.

Example sentences and meaning

1. sparkle, shine

* 彼女の目に涙が光っていた。
  Tears were glistening in her eyes.
* あの光は何かしら。
  I wonder what that light is!

2. scenery-related

* イギリスへは観光旅行で行きました。
  I went to Britain on a sightseeing trip.

3. honor

* レーサーたちは栄光を目指して疾走した。
  With their hopes set on glory, the drivers raced at full speed.

Common compounds

風光	ふうこう	scenery, natural beauty
光熱	こうねつ	light and heat
逆光	ぎゃっこう	backlighting
光景	こうけい	scene, sight
日光	にっこう	sunlight, Nikkō (place)

光 ← stroke hooks up

6　丨　丬　丷　丯　丬　光

光

122

考

コウ
かんが・える

think, consider

考 combines *old person* 耂 and *bent* 丂, a reference to *wisdom* that an old man bent with age has.

Example sentences and meaning

1. think, devise

* それはいい考えだね。
  That's a good idea.
* 最近思考力の衰えを感じるよ。
  Lately I've been finding it hard to concentrate.

2. compare and clarify

* 何かいい参考書はないかな。
  I wonder if there might be any good reference books.
* 私は考古学に興味があります。
  I'm interested in archaeology.

Common compounds

選考	せんこう	selection, choice
熟考	じゅっこう	consideration, deliberation
参考	さんこう	reference, consultation
考案	こうあん	idea, conception, plan
考え過ぎ	かんがえすぎ	think too much

考 ← stroke tapers down from right to left

6　一　十　土　耂　耂　考

考

Quiz 16 (117-122)

A. Match the kanji with its English meaning

1. 羽田空港 ____
2. 次回 ____
3. 社会 ____
4. 交通事故 ____
5. 観光旅行 ____
6. 選考 ____
7. 羽音 ____
8. 回り道 ____

a. sightseeing trip
b. society
c. roundabout way
d. Haneda Airport
e. selection
f. next time
g. traffic accident
h. sound of flapping wings

B. Write in hiragana and katakana

1. 教会 ____________
2. 交際 ____________
3. 光景 ____________
4. 参考書 ____________
5. インコ二羽 ____________
6. 回収 ____________
7. 会議中 ____________
8. 交番 ____________
9. 日光 ____________
10. 考古学 ____________

C. Write in kanji and kana

1. はめ ____ ____
2. こんかい ____ ____
3. かいしゃ ____社
4. こうさ ____差
5. えいこう 栄 ____
6. かんがえすぎ ____ ____ 過 ____
7. もういっかい ____ ____ ____ ____
8. たいかい ____ ____

123 行

コウ、ギョウ
い・く、ゆ・く、おこな・う
go, row, carry out

行 originated from a pictograph of an *intersection* ╋, a point of stopping and *going.*

Example sentences and meaning

1. go

* 学校(がっこう)へ行(い)く
to go to school

* この道(みち)は一方通行(いっぽうつうこう)だ。
This is a one-way street.

2. do

* 試験(しけん)を行(おこな)う
to give an examination

* 手続(てつづ)きを行(おこな)う
to follow a procedure

3. line, row

* 映画館(えいがかん)の前(まえ)に長(なが)い行列(ぎょうれつ)があった。
There was a long line in front of the movie theatre.

Common compounds

急行	きゅうこう	express train
通行	つうこう	passing, traffic
銀行	ぎんこう	bank
代行	だいこう	agent, proxy
*行方	ゆくえ	whereabouts

行 ← stroke longer than one above it
← stroke ends with hook

6 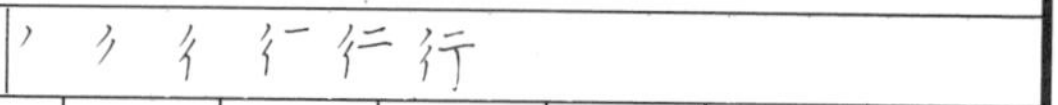

行

124 合

ゴウ、ガッ
あ・う、あ・わす
together, total, combine

合 shows a *lid* and a *bowl* being *put together*.

Example sentences and meaning

1. bring together, be in order

* なかなか意見が合わなかった。
We just couldn't see eye to eye.
* 明日は朝八時に集合して下さい。
Please be there tomorrow morning at 8:00.

2. be suitable

* その服よく似合うよ。
That outfit really suits you!

3. unit indicating one-tenth of the distance up a mountain

* 富士山の五合目までは車で行けます。
You can go up to the fifth station on Mount Fuji by car.

Common compounds

合意	ごうい	mutual consent, agreement
合計	ごうけい	total
合成	ごうせい	synthetic, combined
合理的	ごうりてき	rational, logical
合気道	あいきどう	aikidō

合 middle line does not touch outside strokes

6 丿 人 人 合 合 合

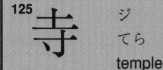

合

125 寺

ジ
てら
temple

寺 combines *hand* 寸 and *foot* 土 and referred to a *place of work*, especially a governmental office. The character later took on the meaning of *temple*.

Example sentences and meaning

1. temple

* 京都にはお寺がたくさんある。
There are many temples in Kyōto.
* 東大寺に日本で一番大きい大仏がある。
The biggest statue of the Buddha in Japan is in the Tōdaiji Temple.

Common compounds

寺院	じいん	temple
山寺	やまでら	mountain temple
寺田	てらだ	Terada (name)
清水寺	きよみずでら	Kiyomizu Temple

stroke longer → 寺 ← stroke ends with hook

6 一 十 土 土 寺 寺

寺

126 自

ジ、シ
みずか・ら
self, by itself

自 depicts the *nose,* which in Japan is a reference to *oneself*.

Example sentences and meaning

1. oneself

* もっと自信を持ちなさい。
Have more confidence in yourself!

2. by oneself

* どうぞご自由にお取り下さい。
Please feel free to help yourself.

* あの人は自立した人ですよ。
He's a very independent person.

3. naturally, of itself, spontaneously

* このままの自然を後生に残したいね。
I'd like nature to be left as it is for future generations.

Common compounds

自宅	じたく	one's home
自殺	じさつ	suicide
自動車	じどうしゃ	motor vehicle, car
自転車	じてんしゃ	bicycle
自給自足	じきゅうじそく	self-sufficiency

自 ← same spacing

6 ′ ′ ′ ′ ′ 自

自

127 色

ショク、シキ
いろ
color

While hard to discern, 色 originally depicted a person bending over another person, i.e., *having sex. Color* perhaps derived from the complexion of the woman.

Example sentences and meaning

1. color, coloration

* どうしたの？顔色が悪いよ。
What's the matter? You look pale!

2. expression, features

* 弟は大学に合格して、喜色満面です。
My younger brother, who got into university, looked absolutely elated.

3. appearance of things

* どこかで見たことのある景色だなあ。
I know I've seen this scene somewhere before.

4. sexual desire

* あの女優はずいぶん色っぽい。
That actress is really sexy.

Common compounds

才色	さいしょく	wit and beauty
無色	むしょく	colorless
原色	げんしょく	primary color
特色	とくしょく	characteristic
保護色	ほごしょく	camouflage

色 ← stroke ends with hook

6 ′ ′ ′ ′ ′ 色

色

128 西

セイ、サイ
にし
west

西 depicted a *bird in a nest*. A bird returns to its nest when the sun sets in the *west*.

Example sentences and meaning

1. west

* 毎日東西線に乗る。
  Every day I take the Tōzai line.
* 西の空に太陽が沈む。
  The sun sets in the western sky.
* この部屋は西日が射して暑い。
  This room is hot from the afternoon sun.

2. Kansai, Western Japan

* 関東より関西の方が好きです。
  I prefer Kansai to Kantō.
* 関西新空港が建設中です。
  The New Kansai Airport is under construction.

Common compounds

西経	せいけい	west longitude
西暦	せいれき	Christian Era, A.D.
北西	ほくせい	northwest
西村	にしむら	Nishimura (name)

西 ← indside right stroke bends

| 6 | 一 | 丆 | 襾 | 两 | 西 | 西 |

西

Test 5 (81-128)

A. Write in kanji and kana
1. いっぽうつうこう ＿＿＿＿ 通＿＿
2. あいきどう ＿＿＿＿ 道
3. とうだいじ 東＿＿＿＿
4. じどうしゃ ＿＿動＿＿
5. むしょく 無＿＿
6. にしむら ＿＿＿＿
7. ようじ ＿＿事
8. たいかい ＿＿＿＿
9. じたく ＿＿宅
10. おにいさん ＿＿＿＿
11. だいほん ＿＿＿＿
12. こうはん 後＿＿
13. きゅうこう 急＿＿
14. いろっぽい ＿＿＿＿
15. ほくせい ＿＿＿＿

B. Write in hiragana
1. 行方 ＿＿＿＿＿＿＿
2. 合理的 ＿＿＿＿＿＿＿
3. 清水寺 ＿＿＿＿＿＿＿
4. 自殺 ＿＿＿＿＿＿＿
5. 特色 ＿＿＿＿＿＿＿
6. 東西線 ＿＿＿＿＿＿＿
7. 会計 ＿＿＿＿＿＿＿
8. 国交 ＿＿＿＿＿＿＿
9. 思考力 ＿＿＿＿＿＿＿
10. 代行 ＿＿＿＿＿＿＿
11. 寺院 ＿＿＿＿＿＿＿
12. 関西新空港 ＿＿＿＿＿＿＿
13. 内外 ＿＿＿＿＿＿＿
14. 用紙 ＿＿＿＿＿＿＿
15. 集合 ＿＿＿＿＿＿＿

C. Write in English
1. 行列 ＿＿＿＿＿＿＿
2. 合計 ＿＿＿＿＿＿＿
3. 山寺 ＿＿＿＿＿＿＿
4. 自然 ＿＿＿＿＿＿＿
5. 顔色 ＿＿＿＿＿＿＿
6. 西暦 ＿＿＿＿＿＿＿
7. 回想 ＿＿＿＿＿＿＿
8. 風光 ＿＿＿＿＿＿＿
9. 合意 ＿＿＿＿＿＿＿
10. 才色 ＿＿＿＿＿＿＿
11. 考古学 ＿＿＿＿＿＿＿

12. 市民センター ＿＿＿＿＿＿＿＿＿
13. 立冬 ＿＿＿＿＿＿＿＿＿
14. 保母さん ＿＿＿＿＿＿＿＿＿
15. 自信 ＿＿＿＿＿＿＿＿＿

D. Match the kanji with its reading
1. 通行 ＿＿＿ a. ひろま
2. 合成 ＿＿＿ b. ふゆもの
3. 寺田 ＿＿＿ c. かんさい
4. 自由 ＿＿＿ d. ほっきょくせい
5. 景色 ＿＿＿ e. とし
6. 関西 ＿＿＿ f. つうこう
7. 意外 ＿＿＿ g. てらだ
8. 古風 ＿＿＿ h. ふぼ
9. 広間 ＿＿＿ i. たかだい
10. 都市 ＿＿＿ j. ごうせい
11. 高台 ＿＿＿ k. けしき
12. 冬物 ＿＿＿ l. いがい
13. 半月 ＿＿＿ m. じゆう
14. 父母 ＿＿＿ n. はんげつ
15. 北極星 ＿＿＿ o. こふう

E. Write in English
1. コートのボタンを外す

＿＿＿＿＿＿＿＿＿＿＿＿＿＿＿

2. お兄さん、古いまんがの本をちょっとかして。

＿＿＿＿＿＿＿＿＿＿＿＿＿＿＿

3. 火事が北の方へ広がった。

＿＿＿＿＿＿＿＿＿＿＿＿＿＿＿

4. 赤い色の矢印

＿＿＿＿＿＿＿＿＿＿＿＿＿＿＿

5. 友だちとあの古いお寺で待ち合わせをした。

＿＿＿＿＿＿＿＿＿＿＿＿＿＿＿

6. 十月の半ごろから冬ふくをきる。

＿＿＿＿＿＿＿＿＿＿＿＿＿＿＿

7. このひょうげんは広く用いられている。

＿＿＿＿＿＿＿＿＿＿＿＿＿＿＿

8. 今朝は古典と化学のテストが行われた。

＿＿＿＿＿＿＿＿＿＿＿＿＿＿＿

9. そのふくの色にそのくつの色は合わない。

10. あなた自ら行ったほうがいい。

_____

F. Fill in the kanji and translate

1. （<ruby>園<rt>こうえん</rt></ruby>）を（<ruby>転<rt>じてんしゃ</rt></ruby>）で（<ruby>　<rt>ふたまわ</rt></ruby>）りした。

2. デパートの（<ruby>　<rt>そと</rt></ruby>）で（<ruby>島<rt>やじま</rt></ruby>）さんに
（<ruby>　<rt>あ</rt></ruby>）った。

3. その（<ruby>　<rt>はね</rt></ruby>）かざりの（<ruby>　<rt>いろ</rt></ruby>）は（<ruby>　<rt>しろ</rt></ruby>）と
（<ruby>　<rt>あか</rt></ruby>）が（<ruby>　<rt>ま</rt></ruby>）じっていた。

4. （<ruby>　<rt>ふたり</rt></ruby>）は（<ruby>　<rt>まち</rt></ruby>）の（<ruby>場<rt>ひろば</rt></ruby>）であいさつを
（<ruby>　<rt>か</rt></ruby>）わした。

5. （<ruby>彼<rt>かのじょ</rt></ruby>）の（<ruby>　<rt>め</rt></ruby>）はなみだで（<ruby>　<rt>ひか</rt></ruby>）っていた。

6. （<ruby>　<rt>しょうねん</rt></ruby>）は（<ruby>　<rt>じぶん</rt></ruby>）のこれからの
（<ruby>　<rt>いきかた</rt></ruby>）について よく（<ruby>　<rt>かんが</rt></ruby>）えた。

7. （<ruby>海道<rt>ほっかいどう</rt></ruby>）へ（<ruby>　<rt>い</rt></ruby>）くためのお（<ruby>　<rt>かね</rt></ruby>）が
（<ruby>　<rt>はんぶん</rt></ruby>）たまった。

8. （<ruby>　<rt>はは</rt></ruby>）といっしょに（<ruby>観<rt>しないかんこう</rt></ruby>）をした。

9. （<ruby>　<rt>にしむら</rt></ruby>）くんのお（<ruby>　<rt>かあ</rt></ruby>）さんは（<ruby>所<rt>だいどころ</rt></ruby>）で
おいしそうなケーキをつくっていた。

10. その（<ruby>　<rt>しろ</rt></ruby>）いとりは（<ruby>　<rt>はね</rt></ruby>）を（<ruby>　<rt>ひろ</rt></ruby>）げて
（<ruby>　<rt>ほくせい</rt></ruby>）の（<ruby>　<rt>ほう</rt></ruby>）へとんでいった。

129

多

タ
おお・い
many, much

多 combines two moons to indicate *many*.

Example sentences and meaning

1. many, numerous

* 最近外食が多い。
  I've been eating out a lot lately.

* ご多忙のところおいで下さってありがとうございます。
  Thank you very much for taking the time to come.

* あちこちでテロが多発している。
  Everywhere you go there is a lot of terrorism.

* 多分明日は雨だね。
  It'll probably rain tomorrow.

Common compounds

多数決	たすうけつ	majority decision
多大	ただい	great amount
多少	たしょう	more or less
多用	たよう	pressure of business
本多	ほんだ	Honda (name)

多 ← bottom half slightly
← larger than top half

6 ノ ク タ タ 多 多

多

130

地

チ、ジ
earth, land

地 combines *soil* 土 and *scorpion* 也 to give the meaning of *earth*.

Example sentences and meaning

1. ground, earth

* 地下鉄は便利ですよ。
  The subway is convenient.

* 地球にやさしい製品
  environmentally-friendly products

2. place, standpoint, position

* 彼は今の地位に満足している。
  He is satisfied with his present position.

3. of that place, region

* 土地の地酒を飲む
  to drink a locally brewed sake

4. one's true character, reality

* 電話の声と地声は全然違いますね。
  You sound completely different on the phone.

Common compounds

土地	とち	land
地方	ちほう	region
天地	てんち	heaven and earth
地図	ちず	map
地獄	じごく	hell

stroke goes up from left to right → 地 ← stroke ends with hook

6 一 十 土 扣 地 地

地

131 池

チ
いけ
pond

池 combines *water* 氵 and *scorpion* 也, which for unclear reasons came to mean *pond*.

Example sentences and meaning

1. **pond, reservoir**
* 池の鯉に餌をやる
  to feed the carp in the pond
* 電池を換えた方がいいよ。
  You'd better change the batteries.
* 貯水池の水が減っている。
  The water in the reservoir is dropping.

Common compounds

古池	ふるいけ	old pond
用水池	ようすいち	reservoir
池田	いけだ	Ikeda (name)
池袋	いけぶくろ	Ikebukuro (place)

池 ← stroke protrudes at left

6 `丶 冫 氵 汁 池 池`

---

132 当

トウ
あ・たる、あ・てる
appropriate, hit, guess at

当 combines *rice field* ヨ (from 田) and *in proportion* ⺌, suggesting that worth was *in proportion to* wealth. From this came the meaning *appropriate* and then *hit*.

Example sentences and meaning

1. **hit, touch**
* ボールがバッターの頭に当たった。
  The ball hit the batter in the head.

2. **take charge of**
* この件の担当はどなたですか。
  Who is in charge of this?

3. **be true of**
* 見当が外れる
  to guess wrong

4. **concerning an issue or subject**
* お金はパーティーの当日持ってきて下さい。
  Please bring the money on the day of the party.

Common compounds

適当	てきとう	suitable, adequate
本当	ほんとう	true, real
当人	とうにん	person involved
割り当て	わりあて	allotment, quota

当 ← top portion not ツ

6 `丨 丬 当 当 当 当`

133 同

ドウ
おな・じ
the same

同 depicts a *plank with a hole* drilled in it. The hole is the *same* size on either side of the plank.

Example sentences and meaning

1. **the same**
* 私たちは同姓同名でよく間違われます。
We have the same family and first names, so people often confuse us.
* 同時通訳でスピーチを聴く
to listen to a speech done in simultaneous translation

2. **make one**
* 二つの会社が合同で会議をした。
The two companies held a joint conference.

3. **a company, party**
* お正月には親戚一同が集まります。
All of the relatives get together for New Year's.

Common compounds

同意	どうい	same meaning or opinion
共同	きょうどう	cooperation, collaboration
同一	どういつ	the same, equal
異同	いどう	difference
同級生	どうきゅうせい	classmate

同 ← stroke ends with hook

6 　｜ 冂 冂 同 同 同

同

134 肉

ニク
meat

肉 depicts a slice of *meat* showing the grains of flesh.

Example sentences and meaning

1. **meat**
* ベジタリアンなので、肉は食べません。
I'm a vegetarian, so I don't eat meat.

2. **something resembling meat**
* このジュースの中には果肉が入っている。
This fruit juice contains pulp.

3. **as it is, direct**
* 肉眼では見えない
to be invisible to the naked eye

4. **blood relationship**
* 彼女は肉親を失った。
She suffered the loss of a relative.

Common compounds

筋肉	きんにく	muscles
牛肉	ぎゅうにく	beef
肉屋	にくや	meat shop
朱肉	しゅにく	red ink pad
皮肉	ひにく	irony, sarcasm

stroke protrudes → 肉 ⇇ end strokes firmly

6 　｜ 冂 内 内 肉 肉

肉

Quiz 17 (129-134)

A. Write in English

1. 多分 _____
2. 地図 _____
3. 貯水池 _____
4. 担当 _____
5. 同級生 _____
6. 肉眼 _____
7. 多数決 _____
8. 天地 _____

B. Write in kanji

1. いけだ ___ ___
2. ほんとう ___ ___
3. ごうどう ___ ___
4. にくや ___屋
5. たしょう ___ ___
6. とち ___ ___
7. でんち 電___
8. けんとう ___ ___
9. どうせいどうめい ___ 姓 ___ ___
10. ぎゅうにく ___ ___

C. Write in hiragana

1. 多発 _____
2. 地球 _____
3. 池袋 _____
4. 割り当て _____
5. 同意 _____
6. 筋肉 _____
7. 本多 _____
8. 地下鉄 _____

135

米

ベイ、マイ
こめ、*よね
rice, America

米 depicts the tip of a *stalk of rice.*

Example sentences and meaning

1. rice

* お米はといでから炊きます。
You cook rice after rinsing it.

2. America, abbreviation for USA

* おみやげは米国製のビーフジャーキー
a gift of American-made beef jerky

* 中南米の音楽が好きです。
I like Latin American music.

3. meter(s)

* 新しい家は百平米あります。
Our new house has an area of one hundred
square meters.

Common compounds

米価	べいか	(government-set) rice price
玄米	げんまい	unmilled (brown) rice
白米	はくまい	polished (white) rice
新米	しんまい	newly harvested rice
米屋	こめや	rice dealer

→ 米 ← strokes slant in

6	丶	ソ	二	半	米	米
米						

136 毎

マイ

every, each

毎 depicts a *mother* 母 wearing a *headpiece* ㇀. The meaning of *every* perhaps stems from the frequency at which the mother gives birth.

Example sentences and meaning

1. always, whenever, each

* 毎日同じことばかり考えている
to think about the same thing every day

* この薬は毎食後にのんで下さい。
Please take this medicine after every meal.

* この番組は毎回おもしろいね。
This program is always interesting.

Common compounds

毎朝	まいあさ	every morning
毎晩	まいばん	every evening, nightly
毎週	まいしゅう	every week, weekly
毎度	まいど	each time, always
毎年	まいねん・まいとし	every year, annually

毎   don't mistake for 母

6   ノ ㇀ 仁 与 勾 毎

毎

137 何

カ

なに、なん

what

何 combines *person* 亻 and *possibility* 可, but its present meaning of *what* derived from phonetic borrowing.

Example sentences and meaning

1. what

* 今何時ですか。
What time is it now?

* 夕食は何がいい？
What would you like to have for dinner?

* 何人ぐらい来る予定ですか。
About how many people are you expecting?

2. entirely, not at all

* それについては何も知りません。
I know nothing about it.

Common compounds

何人	なんにん	how many people
何曜日	なんようび	what day of the week
何日	なんにち	how many days, what day of the month
*何処	どこ	where

何   ← stroke ends with hook

7   ノ 亻 亻 仁 侗 何 何

何

138 角

カク
かど、つの
angle, corner, horn

角 depicts a beast's *horns*.

Example sentences and meaning

1. horn, antlers

* このバックルは水牛の角でできています。
This buckle is made from a water buffalo's horn.

2. angle, corner

*最初の角を右に曲がる
to turn right at the first corner

3. point of intersection

* この紙は直角に切れていない。
This paper hasn't been cut squarely!

4. compare

* 二人の選手は互角だ。
The two players are evenly-matched.

Common compounds

三角	さんかく	triangular
方角	ほうがく	direction
角度	かくど	angle
広角レンズ	こうかくレンズ	wide-angle lens

stroke tapers off → 角 ← stroke ends with hook

7 ﾉ ｱ ｳ 朿 角 角 角

角

139 汽

キ
steam

汽 combines *water* 氵, and *vapor* 气 to give the meaning of *steam*.

Example sentences and meaning

1. vapor, steam

* 今も汽車は観光用に走っている。
Even now, steam trains are used for sightseeing.

* 港のそばなので、汽笛が聞こえる。
Because it's near the harbor, you can hear the ships' whistles.

Common compounds

汽車	きしゃ	steam train
汽船	きせん	steamship
夜汽車	よぎしゃ	night train

汽 ← last stroke not 乙

7 丶 冫 氵 汋 汽 汽 汽

汽

140 近

キン
ちか・い
near

近 combines *movement* 辶 and *axe* 斤 suggesting a *short* movement. From this came the meaning of *near*.

Example sentences and meaning

1. close, near

* 家から駅が近い。
The station is close to my house.

* 学校の近くに本屋がある。
There's a bookshop close to school.

* 最近おもしろい映画見た？
Seen any interesting movies lately?

2. come close, approach

* 台風が日本列島に接近している。
A typhoon is approaching the Japanese Archipelago.

Common compounds

手近	てぢか	familiar, close by, handy
近年	きんねん	in recent years
近郊	きんこう	suburbs, the outskirts
付近	ふきん	neighborhood, vicinity
近畿	きんき	Kinki region

drawn in one stroke → 近 ← end stroke firmly

7　ノ　亅　亅　午　斤　沂　近　近

近

Quiz 18 (135-140)

A. Write in kanji

1. polished (white) rice ＿＿＿ ＿＿＿
2. every morning ＿＿＿朝
3. What time? ＿＿＿時
4. triangular ＿＿＿ ＿＿＿
5. steam train ＿＿＿ ＿＿＿
6. lately, recently 最 ＿＿＿
7. rice dealer ＿＿＿屋
8. every week ＿＿＿週

B. Match the kanji with its reading

1. なんようび ＿＿＿＿　a. 夜汽車
2. ちょっかく ＿＿＿＿　b. 毎度
3. きせん ＿＿＿＿　c. 近年
4. ふきん ＿＿＿＿　d. 直角
5. べいか ＿＿＿＿　e. 何人
6. まいど ＿＿＿＿　f. 何曜日
7. なんにん ＿＿＿＿　g. 米価
8. ほうかく ＿＿＿＿　h. 汽船
9. よぎしゃ ＿＿＿＿　i. 方角
10. きんねん ＿＿＿＿　j. 付近

C. Write in hiragana and katakana

1. 新米 ＿＿＿＿＿＿＿＿
2. 毎食後 ＿＿＿＿＿＿＿＿
3. 何日 ＿＿＿＿＿＿＿＿
4. 広角レンズ ＿＿＿＿＿＿＿
5. 毎回 ＿＿＿＿＿＿＿＿
6. 接近 ＿＿＿＿＿＿＿＿
7. 米国製 ＿＿＿＿＿＿＿＿
8. 毎晩 ＿＿＿＿＿＿＿＿

141 形

ケイ、ギョウ
かたち、かた
form, shape

形 depicts a window with a *grid pattern* 开 and *brushwork* 彡, suggesting *copying a pattern*.

Example sentences and meaning

1. form, shape

* 形のおもしろい石を集める
  to collect stones with interesting shapes
* 紙を三角形に折る
  to fold paper into a triangular shape

2. shape, mold

* プラスチックを金型で成形する
  to shape plastic in a metal mold

3. situation

* この辺は地形が複雑です。
  The topography of this area is complex.

Common compounds

円形	えんけい	round shape, circle
形式	けいしき	formality
形容詞	けいようし	adjective
形見	かたみ	keepsake
人形	にんぎょう	doll

stroke longer than one above it → 形

7 一 二 テ 开 形 形 形

形

142 言

ゲン、ゴン
い・う、こと
word, say

言 depicted a *knife* pointing down at a *mouth,* suggesting the clear-cut pronunciation of sounds to form *words*.

Example sentences and meaning

1. say

* もう一度言って下さい。
  Please say that again.
* 裁判で証言する
  to give evidence at a trial

2. words, language

* 大学で言語学を専攻した。
  I majored in linguistics at university.
* 遺言を書いておく
  to draw up a will

Common compounds

言葉	ことば	word, language, expression
予言	よげん	prediction
方言	ほうげん	dialect
名言	めいげん	wise saying
発言	はつげん	speech, proposal

言 ← this stroke longest

7 ` 一 二 三 言 言 言

言

143 谷

コク
たに、*や
valley, ravine, canyon

谷 depicts *splitting* 八 and *opening* 口, a reference to a *valley*.

Example sentences and meaning

1. **valley, ravine**
* 谷川を下る
to go down a mountain stream
* ビルの谷間に小さな公園がある。
There's a little park between the buildings.

Common compounds

谷川	たにがわ	mountain stream
大渓谷	だいけいこく	large canyon
渋谷	しぶや	Shibuya (place)
小谷	こたに	Kotani (name)

→ 谷 ← strokes taper off

7 ′ ハ グ 父 父 谷 谷

谷

144 作

サク、サ
つく・る
work, production, make

作 combines *person* イ and *construct* 乍 to give the meaning of *make*.

Example sentences and meaning

1. **make**
* 今日はカレーを作ろう。
I'll make curry today.
* テレビ番組を制作する
to produce a television program

2. **something made**
* この作品は名作ですよ。
This work is a masterpiece.

3. **job**
* 編集作業がなかなか進まない。
I haven't made much editorial progress.

4. **action, movement**
* この薬は眠くなる作用がありますか。
Will this medicine make me drowsy?

Common compounds

作文	さくぶん	composition, writing
工作	こうさく	construction, engineering
動作	どうさ	action, motion
作法	さほう	manners, etiquette
作曲家	さっきょくか	musical composer

作 ← stroke longer than those below it

7 ノ イ イ 作 作 作 作

作

145 社

シャ
やしろ
company, Shinto shrine

社 combines *ground* 土 and *altar* ネ, the makings of a *shrine*.

Example sentences and meaning

1. the world

* 未開の社会を調べる
to do research on primitive societies

2. company, organization

* 仲間と三人で小さな会社を作った。
Two colleagues and myself formed a small company.

* 去年の四月に入社しました。
I joined a firm in April of last year.

3. Shinto shrine

* 神社にお参りに行く
to visit a Shinto shrine

Common compounds

社交	しゃこう	social life
本社	ほんしゃ	head office
支社	ししゃ	branch office
商社	しょうしゃ	trading company
社長	しゃちょう	company president

社　　this stroke longer
← than one above it

7 ` ク ネ ネー 社 社

社

146 図

ズ、ト
はか・る
drawing, diagram, plan

図 combines *enclosure* □ and a very stylized pictograph of a *field* メ, suggesting an enclosed area drawn on a *map*.

Example sentences and meaning

1. draw, a book

* 地図を見る
to look at a map

* 図書館で調べものをする
to do research in the library

2. think, propose, idea, undertaking

* どうも彼の意図がはっきりしない。
What he intends to do just isn't clear.

* 用意ができたら合図して下さい。
Please indicate when you are ready.

Common compounds

図形	ずけい	diagram, figure
設計図	せっけいず	plan, blueprint
天気図	てんきず	weather map
図星	ずぼし	the bull's eye

図 ← end sixth stroke firmly

7 丨 冂 冂 冋 冈 図 図

図

Quiz 19 (141-146)

A. Write in English

1. 三角形 _____
2. 予言 _____
3. 谷川 _____
4. 名作 _____
5. 社会 _____
6. 合図 _____
7. 形式 _____
8. 遺言 _____

C. Write in hiragana

1. 円形 _____
2. 発言 _____
3. 大渓谷 _____
4. 作業 _____
5. 神社 _____
6. 図書館 _____
7. 形容詞 _____
8. 言語学 _____

B. Write in kanji

1. しぶや　　　渋___
2. さくぶん　　___ ___
3. にゅうしゃ　___ ___
4. てんきず　　___ ___ ___
5. にんぎょう　___ ___
6. ことば　　　___葉
7. こたに　　　
8. さくひん　　___品
9. しゃちょう　___ ___
10. ちず　　　　___ ___

---

147 声　セイ、*ショウ
　　　こえ、*こわ
　　　voice

声 derived from a pictograph of an *instrument* made up of suspended stones. *Voice* came from its former meaning of *sound*.

Example sentences and meaning

1. voice

* 電話の声はいつもの声と違うね。
  Your voice on the telephone sounds different from your real voice.
* そんな大声を出さないで。
  Stop yelling!

2. speak, say something

* 首相は声明を発表した。
  The prime minister made an official statement.

3. reputation, honor

* 彼はデザイナーとしての名声を得た。
  He gained fame as a designer.

Common compounds

音声	おんせい	voice, audio
名声	めいせい	reputation
声帯	せいたい	vocal cords
声価	せいか	reputation, fame
*声色	こわいろ	tone of voice, mimicry

声　← this stroke shorter than one above it
stroke tapers off →

7　一 十 士 声 声 声 声

声

148 走　ソウ　はし・る　run

走 depicts a *person running,* taking long strides and with arms outstretched.

Example sentences and meaning

1. run, vehicles moving

* 百メートルを十一秒で走った。
I ran the one hundred meters in 11 seconds.

* 車が暴走してけが人が出た。
People were injured because the car was being driven recklessly.

* 飛行機が滑走しはじめた。
The airplane began to taxi out.

2. escape

* 銀行強盗はまだ逃走中です。
The bank robber is still at large.

Common compounds

滑走路	かっそうろ	runway
脱走	だっそう	escape, flee
小走り	こばしり	run with short steps
走行距離	そうこうきょり	distance covered, mileage
*師走	しわす	year-end, December

this stroke longer → 走
than one above it

7　一 十 土 キ キ 走 走

走

149 体　タイ、テイ　からだ　body, object

体 combines *person* イ and *foundation* 本 suggesting that the foundation of a person is the *body.*

Example sentences and meaning

1. body

* 一日中テニスをしたら体中が痛くなった。
After playing tennis all day, I ached all over.

* 体重を量る
to weigh oneself

2. shape, appearance, essence

* この作家は独特の文体を持っている。
This writer has a distinctive literary style.

* 世間体ばかり気にしていては何もできない。
If you keep worrying about what other people think, you won't be able to get anything done.

3. acquire, physically take in

* 外国生活を体験したい。
I want to experience life abroad.

Common compounds

体操	たいそう	gymnastics, calisthenics
大体	だいたい	generally, on the whole
死体	したい	corpse
本体	ほんたい	substance, true form
体当たり	たいあたり	hurl oneself against

体　end strokes firmly

7　ノ イ イ 什 休 体 体

体

150 弟

テイ、*ダイ、*デ
おとうと
younger brother, pupil, disciple

弟 depicted *stakes bound with twine.* The lower ノ represents *low,* and from this came *younger brother,* who is low in position and short in height.

Example sentences and meaning

1. younger brother

* 四つ違いの弟がいます。
I have a brother who is four years younger than me.

* 兄弟げんかはやめなさい。
Stop fighting with your brother!

2. pupil, disciple

* あの先生には三十人の弟子がいる。
That teacher has 30 pupils.

* あの二人は師弟でもあり友人でもある。
The two of them are master and pupil as well as friends.

Common compounds

師弟	してい	master and pupil
子弟	してい	children
徒弟	とてい	apprentice
高弟	こうてい	one's best student

弟 ← stroke ends with hook

7 `丶 ヽ ソ ゝ 弓 弟 弟`

弟

151 売

バイ
う・る
sell

売 combines *put out* 士 (from 出) and 儿 *buy* (from 買). *Sell* comes from the idea of *put out* for *buying.*

Example sentences and meaning

1. sell, be in demand

* あの店では切手も売っている。
They also sell stamps at that store.

* この雑誌は毎週水曜日発売です。
This magazine goes on sale every Wednesday.

2. betray

* 情報をライバル会社に売る
to leak information to a rival company

3. publicize, become famous

* あの子は今売り出し中の歌手です。
That girl is an up-and-coming singer.

Common compounds

前売り	まえうり	advance sale
安売り	やすうり	sell cheaply, bargain sale
販売	はんばい	sales, selling
売り物	うりもの	things for sale
売店	ばいてん	newsstand, kiosk

this stroke longer → 売
than one below it   ← stroke ends with hook

7 `一 十 士 声 声 声 売`

売

152 麦

バク
むぎ
wheat, barley, rye, oats

麦 combines *stalk of wheat* 𡗗 and *foot* 夂, in reference to people carrying *wheat* from distant places.

Example sentences and meaning

1. wheat, barley, rye, oats

* 小麦粉と卵、牛乳でケーキを焼く
  to bake a cake using flour, eggs, and milk

* 夏は麦茶がおいしい。
  Barley tea is delicious in summer.

* このビールは麦芽百パーセントだ。
  This is one hundred percent malt beer.

* ライ麦畑でつかまえて
  The Catcher in the Rye

Common compounds

大麦	おおむぎ	barley
小麦	こむぎ	wheat
麦畑	むぎばたけ	wheat field
生麦	なまむぎ	raw wheat

麦 ← bottom portion not 又

7　一 十 キ キ 主 麦 麦

麦

Test 6

Test 6 (81-152)

A. Write in Kanji and kana

1. audio, voice ___ ___
2. run with short steps ___ ___ ___
3. on the whole, generally ___ ___
4. pupil, disciple ___ ___
5. advance sale 前 ___ ___
6. wheat ___ ___
7. low voice, whisper 低 ___
8. hell ___ 獄
9. every day ___ ___
10. how many hours? ___ 時間
11. head office ___ ___
12. map ___ ___
13. dialect ___ ___
14. every year ___ ___
15. going out ___ ___
16. one's native country ___ ___
17. Nikkō ___ ___
18. mayor ___ ___
19. center of gravity 重 ___
20. log ___ ___

B. Write in hiragana

1. 声帯 _____
2. 滑走路 _____
3. 体験 _____
4. 徒弟 _____
5. 売り出し中 _____
6. 麦畑 _____
7. 売り上げ _____
8. 多用 _____
9. 当人 _____
10. 肉親 _____
11. 汽笛 _____
12. 谷間 _____
13. 共同 _____
14. 毎回 _____
15. 名言 _____
16. 用意 _____
17. 参考 _____
18. 交友 _____
19. 回り道 _____
20. 今回 _____

C. Write in kanji

1. おおごえ ___ ___
2. だっそう 脱 ___
3. からだじゅう ___ ___

4. きょうだい ___ ___
5. やすうり 安 ___ ___
6. なまむぎ ___ ___
7. ばいてん ___ 店
8. ちほう ___ ___
9. にひゃくへいべい ___ ___ 平 ___
10. てぢか ___ ___
11. げんごがく ___ 語 ___
12. こうさく ___ ___
13. かいしゃ ___ ___
14. おおむぎ ___ ___
15. たいじゅう ___ 重
16. ふるほんや ___ ___ 屋
17. ろくじはん ___ 時 ___
18. ペキン ___ 京
19. しゃかい ___ ___
20. やじるし ___ 印

D. Match the kanji with its reading

1. 声価 ___   a. こむぎこ
2. 逃走中 ___   b. ようすいち
3. 体操 ___   c. さっきょくか
4. 師弟 ___   d. かにく
5. 発売 ___   e. せいか
6. 小麦粉 ___   f. ししゃ
7. 走行距離 ___   g. どうさ
8. 死体 ___   h. せんよう
9. 用水池 ___   i. たいそう
10. 同時通訳 ___   j. したい
11. 形見 ___   k. ずけい
12. 作曲家 ___   l. とうそうちゅう
13. 図形 ___   m. いと
14. 動作 ___   n. しょうしゃ
15. 商社 ___   o. はつばい
16. 果肉 ___   p. かたみ
17. 支社 ___   q. そうこうきょり
18. 意図 ___   r. ぶたい
19. 舞台 ___   s. どうじつうやく
20. 専用 ___   t. してい

E. Rewrite using as many kanji as possible

1. こたにさん の いぬ は いけ の ま わり を はしっている。

_____

2. まいにち おなじ ライむぎパン の サ

ンドイッチ を たべる と あきます
ね。

_____

3. きみ の おとうとさん、なに を つ
くってる の。 あ、きしゃ か。

_____

4. はじめて にほん に きた ゆうじん
が おどろいて、「ひとがおおいね」とお
おごえ で いった。

_____

5. 「すみません、にく を うっている お
みせ が この ちかく に あります
か。」

_____

「はい、あそこ の かど に スーパー
が あります よ。」

_____

6. ボール が よねやまさん の あし に
あたった。

_____

7. あいず を したら いけ の そば の
やしろ の ところ まで はしりなさ
い。

_____

8. いけたにさん の からだ と わたし
の からだ は おなじ よう な かた
ち を している。

_____

9. にしかわさん は じぶん の たんぼ
で おこめ を つくっている。

_____

10. さくじつ、うち の きんじょ で わか
い じょせい が じさつ を はかった。

_____

153 来

ライ

く・る、きた・す

come, cause, bring about

来 derived from a pictograph of *wheat*. The meaning of *come* perhaps was connected with wheat having been *brought* from a distant country.

Example sentences and meaning

1. **come, visit, approach**
   * 電車が来た。
   The train's arrived.

2. **what is to come, the very next**
   * 未来のことはだれも知らない。
   No one knows what the future holds.

3. **up until the present**
   * お正月以来会っていませんね。
   We haven't seen each other since New Year's.

4. **bring about a certain result, lead to**
   * コンピューターがダウンして仕事に支障を来した。
   Because the computer was down, my work was hindered.

Common compounds

来日	らいにち	come to Japan
来店	らいてん	come to a store
元来	がんらい	originally, by nature
由来	ゆらい	origin, derived from
来月	らいげつ	next month

来 ← this stroke longer than one above it

7 一 ㇒ ㇇ 立 歺 来 来

来

154 里

リ

さと

village, hamlet

里 combines *field* 田 and *earth* 土, indicating an area of land where people lived, i.e., a *village*.

Example sentences and meaning

1. **group of dwellings, village**
   * 食べ物を求めて熊が里に下りてきた。
   Looking for food, the bears came down into the village.

2. **one's birthplace**
   * 郷里の素朴な料理が懐かしい。
   I miss the simple cooking of my hometown.

3. **foster parent**
   * 私はフィリピンの子供の里親になった。
   I became a foster-parent to a Filipino child.

4. **ancient unit of distance, 1 *ri* = 3.9 km**
   * 万里の長城
   Great Wall of China

Common compounds

里心	さとごころ	homesickness, nostalgia
里子	さとご	foster child
海里	かいり	nautical mile
村里	むらざと	villages
首里	しゅり	Shuri (place)

stroke longer than one above it → 里

7 丨 冂 冃 日 甲 里 里

里

155 画　ガ、カク
picture, drawing, kanji stroke

画 shows a *hand* holding a *brush* 一, over a *rice paddy* 田 that is surrounded by a *partition* 凵. This suggested dividing fields with a brush, which then came to mean *draw*.

Example sentences and meaning

1. picture, draw, image

* 将来は画家になりたい。
I'd like to become an artist in the future.

* 映画を見に行かない？
Would you like to go see a movie?

2. divide, draw a line, limit

* 街の区画整理
readjustment of town lots

3. plan, carry out a scheme

* 旅行の計画はありますか。
Do you have any travel plans?

4. kanji stroke

* 「字」の画数は六画です。
The character 字 has six strokes.

Common compounds

版画	はんが	woodblock print
漫画	まんが	cartoon, comics
録画	ろくが	videotape recording
画策	かくさく	plan, map out, scheme
画一的	かくいつてき	uniform, standard

画　central vertical stroke does not protrude

8　一　亠　开　币　雨　甶　画　画

画

---

156 岩　ガン　いわ
rock

岩 combines *mountain* 山 and *stone* 石 to suggest large *rocks*.

Example sentences and meaning

1. rock

* 火山から溶岩が流れ出した。
Lava began to flow from the volcano.

* その山はごつごつした岩山で木がほとんどない。
That mountain is rugged and has hardly any trees on it.

Common compounds

岩石	がんせき	rock
削岩機	さくがんき	jackhammer
岩塩	がんえん	rock salt
岩手県	いわてけん	Iwate Prefecture (place)

岩　← top portion much shorter than bottom portion

8　丿　屮　山　屮　户　岩　岩　岩

岩

157 京 キョウ、ケイ capital

京 derived from a pictograph of a *house on a hill,* a reference to the residences of nobles, who spent much of their time in the *capital.*

Example sentences and meaning

1. **capital, metropolis**
   * 上京して十年たつ。
   Ten years have passed since I came to Tōkyō.

2. **abbreviation for 東京 (Tōkyō)**
   * 京浜高速を使って家へ帰る
   to go back home using the Keihin (Tōkyō–Yokohama) Expressway

3. **abbreviation for 京都 (Kyōto)**
   * 妻の料理は京風の味付けだ。
   My wife uses Kyōto-style seasoning in her cooking.
   * 兄は京大を去年卒業した。
   My elder brother graduated from University of Kyōto last year.

Common compounds

東京	とうきょう	Tōkyō
京阪	けいはん	Kyōto-Ōsaka area
京都	きょうと	Kyōto
京劇	きょうげき	Peking Opera

this stroke longer → 京 middle stroke ends
than those below it ← with hook

8 ′ 亠 亠 亠 宁 宁 京 京

158 国 コク くに country

国 combines *jewels* 玉 and *enclosure* 囗, suggesting that a *country* is a land of treasures.

Example sentences and meaning

1. **country**
   * 国際会議に出席する
   to attend an international conference
   * 日光国立公園に行く
   to go to Nikkō National Park

2. **the Japanese nation**
   * 国産の車に乗っています。
   I drive a Japanese-made car.
   * 国語の授業は好きだった。
   I liked the Japanese language classes.

3. **one's home, native place**
   * お国はどちらですか。
   Where are you from?

Common compounds

国土	こくど	territory, country
国民	こくみん	the people, a national
国境	こっきょう	border, national boundary
国連	こくれん	United Nations
国籍	こくせき	nationality, citizenship

国 ← don't forget dot

8 丨 冂 冂 厅 用 囯 国 国

159 姉

シ
あね
elder sister

姉 combines *woman* 女 and *city* 市, which was borrowed for phonetic reasons.

Example sentences and meaning

1. elder sister

* あそこの姉妹はよく似ていますね。
  Those sisters look alike, don't they?

* 三つ上の姉がいる。
  I have a sister who is three years older than me.

* お姉さん、ちょっとこれ貸して。
  Lend me this, will you? (said to older sister)

2. formal word used with women to indicate familiarity, respect

* 諸姉のご健闘をお祈りします。
  Good luck to you, ladies!

Common compounds

姉妹都市	しまいとし	sister city
姉妹品	しまいひん	companion product
長姉	ちょうし	eldest daughter

written in one stroke → 姉 ← stroke ends with hook

8 　く　女　女　女'　女'　女'　女'　姉

姉

160 知

チ
し・る、し・らせる
know, notify, inform

知 combines *mouth* 口 and *arrow* 矢, suggesting *straightfoward* answers are a sign of *wisdom*.

Example sentences and meaning

1. know, understand, knowledge

* 新聞でその事件を知った。
  I learned of that incident from the newspaper.

* 化学の知識はあまりないんです。
  I don't know much about chemistry.

2. be an acquaintance of

* 彼とはパーティーで知り合いました。
  I got to know him at a party.

3. inform, notification

* 試験の結果は郵便で通知します。
  We will notify you of your exam results by mail.

Common compounds

知恵	ちえ	knowledge, intelligence
感知	かんち	perception, sensing
無知	むち	ignorance
知事	ちじ	governor
知人	ちじん	acquaintance

知 ← end last stroke of 矢 firmly

8 　ノ　ト　ヒ　午　矢　知　知　知

知

Quiz 20 (153-160)

A. Match the kanji with its English meaning

1.	来日	___	a.	Iwate Prefecture
2.	村里	___	b.	eldest daughter
3.	映画	___	c.	come to Japan
4.	岩手県	___	d.	ignorance
5.	京都	___	e.	nationality
6.	国籍	___	f.	movie
7.	長姉	___	g.	Kyōto
8.	無知	___	h.	villages

B. Write in hiragana

1. 来月 _____
2. 万里の長城 _____
3. 計画 _____
4. 溶岩 _____
5. 京阪 _____
6. 国連 _____
7. お姉さん _____
8. 知事 _____
9. 以来 _____
10. 里心 _____

C. Write in kanji

1. がか _____ 家
2. がんせき _____ _____
3. とうきょう 東 _____
4. こくりつこうえん _____ _____ _____ 園
5. しまい _____ 妹
6. ちじん _____ _____
7. らいてん _____ 店
8. ろくが 録 _____

Review Test 2 (81-160)

A. Write in hiragana

1. 由来 _____
2. 里親 _____
3. 漫画 _____
4. 岩山 _____
5. 京大 _____
6. 国産 _____
7. 姉妹都市 _____
8. 通知 _____
9. 丸ごと _____
10. 工業 _____
11. 万葉集 _____
12. 取引 _____
13. 根元 _____
14. 一戸建ての家 _____
15. 感心 _____
16. 古川 _____
17. 台湾 _____
18. 作用 _____
19. 羽田空港 _____
20. 回覧 _____

B. Write in English

1. 未来 _____
2. 里子 _____
3. 画一的 _____
4. 岩塩 _____
5. 上京 _____
6. 国語 _____
7. 姉妹品 _____
8. 無知 _____
9. 商才 _____
10. 公共 _____
11. 休止 _____
12. 減少 _____
13. 太刀 _____
14. 市況 _____
15. 冬季オリンピック _____
16. 半島 _____
17. 迂回 _____
18. 光熱 _____
19. 選考 _____
20. 多大 _____

C. Write in kanji and kana

1. こくご ____語
2. おねえさん ____ ____ ____ ____

3. ぎゅうかわ ____革
4. じもと ____ ____
5. いっさい ____ ____
6. がいけん ____ ____
7. くじはん ____時____
8. ほっかいどう ____海道
9. まわりみち ____ ____道
10. こうばん ____番
11. じざけ ____酒
12. いけだ ____ ____
13. ちゅうなんべい ____南____
14. まいあさ ____朝
15. すいぎゅうのつの ____ ____ ____
16. きしゃ ____ ____
17. ふきん 付____
18. にんぎょう ____ ____
19. ほうげん ____ ____
20. こたに ____ ____

D. Write in kanji and kana

1. Japanese sword ____ ____ ____
2. bow and arrow ____ ____
3. two P.M. ____後____時
4. fairness, justice ____義
5. this year ____ ____
6. brothers (and sisters) ____ ____
7. Hiroshima ____島
8. kitchen ____所
9. mother and father ____ ____
10. facing north ____向
11. urgent business 急____
12. church 教____
13. Nikkō ____ ____
14. maybe, perhaps ____ ____
15. heaven and earth ____ ____
16. battery 電____
17. true, real ____ ____
18. beef ____ ____
19. rice dealer ____屋
20. what day of the month? ____ ____

E. Match the kanji with its reading

1. 渋谷 ____ a. がんらい
2. 作法 ____ b. しぶや
3. 社交 ____ c. にあう
4. 設計図 ____ d. だっそう
5. 元来 ____ e. こむぎこ

6. 内閣 _____ f. しんゆう
7. 十五分 _____ g. さほう
8. 方法 _____ h. くさわけ
9. 読み方 _____ i. ほんたい
10. 毛深い _____ j. せっけいず
11. 親友 _____ k. じゅうごふん
12. 似合う _____ l. しゃこう
13. 自給自足 _____ m. かない
14. 関西 _____ n. ないかく
15. 脱走 _____ o. はんばい
16. 本体 _____ p. じきゅうじそく
17. 販売 _____ q. よみかた
18. 小麦粉 _____ r. ほうほう
19. 家内 _____ s. かんさい
20. 草分け _____ t. けぶかい

F. Match the kanji with its English meaning

1. 悪友 _____ a. temple
2. 一方通行 _____ b. official statement
3. 寺院 _____ c. priest, father
4. 自転車 _____ d. hair
5. 原色 _____ e. bad company
6. 声明 _____ f. nautical mile
7. 大体 _____ g. accounting, the bill
8. 子弟 _____ h. one-way traffic
9. 内閣 _____ i. next month
10. 神父 _____ j. part
11. 部分 _____ k. generally
12. 味方 _____ l. bicycle
13. 髪の毛 _____ m. independent
14. 級友 _____ n. eyebrows
15. 夕方 _____ o. children
16. 眉毛 _____ p. classmate
17. 会計 _____ q. the Cabinet
18. 自立 _____ r. evening
19. 来月 _____ s. primary color
20. 海里 _____ t. friend, ally

G. Rewrite using as many kanji as possible

1. 「いつ とうきょう に きた の です か。」

　　_____

　「きょう の ごご、あね と いっしょ に きました。」

　　_____

2. 「くに は どちら です か。」

　　_____

　「ちゅうごくの ペキン と いう とこ ろ から きました。」

　　_____

3. 「いわたくん を しっています か。」

　　_____

　「からだ が ほそくて、め が まるく て おおきい こ です ね。」

　　_____

4. むらかみさん は こえ が ちいさく て、いま なに を いった か わから ない。

　　_____

5. その ふるい おてら の ちかく で おこめ と おおむぎ を やすく うっ ている みせ が ある そう です。

　　_____

6. たぶん みょうにち はは と おとうと は ひろしま の へいわきねん こうえ ん を み に いきます。

　　_____

7. かみ の け を きって もらって、す こし して から、とたにさん と あっ た。

　　_____

8. きょう は もう よう が ない か ら、まち の いけ の そば の あき ち で キャッチ ボール を しよう。

　　_____

9. はねだ から しながわ まで、ちず を みないで じてんしゃ で いちじかん じゅっぷん で こられた。

　　_____

10. ことし の ふゆ の りゅうこう の いろ は くろ な ので、あなた の よう な いろじろ の ひと に は にあう でしょう。

161 長

チョウ
なが・い
long

長 derived from a pictograph of a *long-haired old man* with a walking stick, suggesting a *long* passage of time.

Example sentences and meaning

1. **long**
   * 部長はいつも話が長い。
   The department chief is always long-winded.

2. **extend, increase, grow up**
   * 子供の成長が楽しみです。
   I enjoy watching the children grow up.

3. **something of excellence**
   * この製品の特長は小さいことです。
   This product's best feature is its compactness.

4. **head, director**
   * 社長からお電話です。
   The company president is on the line.

Common compounds

長短	ちょうたん	strength and weakness
長期	ちょうき	long-term, long-range
身長	しんちょう	one's height
長年	ながねん	many years, a long time
店長	てんちょう	store manager

stroke ends with hook → 長 ← this stroke longer

8　｜　厂　厂　F　E　E　長　長　長

長

162 直

チョク、ジキ
ただ・ちに、なお・す
straight, direct, immediately, fix

直 combines *direct* ⼇, *eye* 目, and *hidden* ∟, suggesting taking a *direct* look at something concealed.

Example sentences and meaning

1. **straight**
   * 直線を引く
   to draw a straight line
   * 赤道直下の国
   countries on the equator

2. **gentle, frank**
   * あの人は正直な人ですよ。
   He's an honest kind of person.

3. **immediately, directly**
   * 彼と直接話して下さい。
   Please speak to him directly.

4. **fix, correct**
   * 日本語の発音を直す
   to correct one's Japanese pronunciation

Common compounds

仲直り	なかなおり	reconciliation
直感	ちょっかん	intuition
直後	ちょくご	immediately after
直角	ちょっかく	right angle
直子	なおこ	Naoko (name)

stroke bends sharply → 直

8　一　十　十　ナ　冇　冇　盲　盲　直

直

163 店

テン
みせ、*たな
shop, store

店 combines *roof* 广 and *arrange* 占, suggesting a *place where objects are arranged and sold;* i.e., a *shop.*

Example sentences and meaning

1. shop, store

* 売店で新聞を買った。
I bought a newspaper at the kiosk.
* 閉店は七時です。
The store closes at 7:00.
* 私は広告代理店に勤めています。
I work for an advertising agency.

Common compounds

本店	ほんてん	main store
喫茶店	きっさてん	café
店長	てんちょう	store manager
店員	てんいん	store employee
開店	かいてん	opening a store

店   inside portion not 古

8 ` 亠 广 广 庐 庐 店 店

店

164 東

トウ
ひがし
east

東 combines *tree* 木 and *sun* 日, representing the morning sun rising in the *east* behind some tree branches.

Example sentences and meaning

1. east

* シルクロードの東の果てが日本です。
The eastern end of the Silk Road is Japan.
* 中東に長く住んでいました。
I lived in the Middle East for a long time.

2. Asia

* 東洋といっても様々な文化があります。
The Orient actually consists of many cultures.

3. Eastern Japan

* 関東地方のニュースをお伝えします。
And now for the Kantō regional news . . .

4. abbreviation of 東京 (Tōkyō)

* 東名高速
Tōmei (Tōkyō–Nagoya) Expressway

Common compounds

東北	とうほく	Tōhoku region
東海	とうかい	eastern sea, the Pacific
東経	とうけい	east longitude

end stroke firmly   → 東 ←   strokes taper off

8 一 厂 厅 百 百 亩 東 東

東

165 歩

ホ、ブ、＊フ
ある・く
step, rate, walk

歩 can be thought of as *foot* 止 and *few* 少, indicating the distance of one *walking stride.*

Example sentences and meaning

1. walk, rate of progress

＊駅まで歩いて十分かかります。
It's a ten-minute walk to the station.

＊進歩しても分からないことは多い。
In spite of progress, many things remain unknown.

2. rate of advantage or disadvantage

＊このままでは私たちに歩がない。
The way things are, we stand little chance of winning.

3. proportion, rate

＊セールスマンの給料は歩合制です。
A salesman earns his salary by commission.

Common compounds

散歩	さんぽ	a walk, stroll
歩道	ほどう	sidewalk
徒歩	とほ	walking
一歩	いっぽ	a step
歩行	ほこう	walking, a walk

歩 ← top portion not 上

stroke tapers off →

| 8 | 丶 | ⻌ | ⺆ | 止 | 牛 | 屮 | 歩 | 歩 |

歩

166 妹

マイ
いもうと
younger sister

妹 combines *woman* 女 and *immature* 未 to mean *younger sister.*

Example sentences and meaning

1. younger sister

＊義理の妹は東京に住んでいます。
My sister-in-law lives in Tōkyō.

＊かわいい妹さんですね。
Your younger sister is cute.

＊あの姉妹は本当に仲がいい。
Those sisters really get along well.

Common compounds

| 姉妹 | しまい | sisters |
| ＊妹尾 | せのお | Senō (name) |

妹 ← this stroke longer than one above it

| 8 | 乀 | 夕 | 女 | 女 | 女̄ | 妌 | 妹 | 妹 |

妹

Quiz 21 (161-166)

A. Write in hiragana
1. 特長 _____
2. 直線 _____
3. 閉店 _____
4. 関東地方 _____
5. 進歩 _____
6. 姉妹 _____
7. 長年 _____
8. 仲直り _____

C. Write in English
1. 身長 _____
2. 直角 _____
3. 中東 _____
4. 東海 _____
5. 散歩 _____
6. 義理の妹 _____
7. 長期 _____
8. 直接 _____

B. Write in kanji
1. ほんてん ___ ___
2. ちゅうとう ___ ___
3. いっぽ ___ ___
4. なおこ ___ ___
5. てんちょう ___ ___
6. しょうじき ___ ___
7. ばいてん ___ ___
8. とうよう ___洋
9. ほどう ___道
10. いもうとさん ___ ___ ___

---

167 明

メイ、ミョウ
あか・るい、あき・らか、
あ・く、あ・かす

light, clear, pass (the night),

明 combines *sun* 日 and *moon* 月, both of which represent *light*.

Example sentences and meaning

1. **light, bright, become light**
   * ちょっと明かりをつけてくれる？
   Would you please turn the light on?

2. **clarify**
   * 英語の説明書ありますか。
   Do you have a manual in English?

3. **day dawns, a crack develops**
   * 明け方はまだ少し寒いね。
   It's still a little cold at dawn.

4. **the next**
   * 明日の十時に伺います。
   I'll visit at 10:00 tomorrow.

Common compounds

証明	しょうめい	proof, certification
声明	せいめい	declaration, public statement
不明	ふめい	unclear, unknown
発明	はつめい	invention
梅雨明け	つゆあけ	end of rainy season

明 ⇐ same spacing

8 ｜ 冂 月 日 日 明 明 明

明

168 門
モン
かど
gate

門 depicts a *double door* that is closed.

Example sentences and meaning

1. gate

* 門をちゃんと閉めて。
  Make sure you shut the gate!
* 池の水門を開けて放水する
  to open the pond's sluice gate to drain the water

2. house, lineage

* 彼は名門の出だ。
  He comes from a distinguished family.

3. same religion, academic

* 私は田中先生の門下生でした。
  I was a pupil of Professor Tanaka.

4. term of classification

* 囲碁の入門書がありますか。
  Do you have an introductory book on *go*?

Common compounds

正門	せいもん	front gate, main entrance
門出	かどで	depart, set out
肛門	こうもん	the anus
仏門	ぶつもん	Buddhism, priesthood
専門	せんもん	specialty

end stroke firmly → 門 ← stroke ends with hook

8 　丨　冂　冃　冃　門　門　門　門

門

---

169 夜
ヤ
よ、よる
night

Although originally derived from different characters, 夜 now combines *person* イ, *roof* 亠, and *evening* 夂, suggesting a person inside at *night*.

Example sentences and meaning

1. night

* 大学の夜間部に通う
  to attend evening sessions of a university
* 夜行列車でスキーに出かける
  to take an overnight train to go skiing
* 夜中に変な電話がかかってきた。
  I got a strange phone call in the middle of the night.
* コアラは夜行性です。
  Koalas are nocturnal.
* ビクトリアピークから見る香港の夜景
  the night view of Hong Kong from Victoria Peak

Common compounds

昨夜	さくや	last night
深夜	しんや	late at night
通夜	つや	a wake, vigil
白夜	びゃくや	white night (in the arctic)

夜 ← make strokes cross

8 　亠　亠　宀　庁　夜　夜　夜

夜

170 科

カ
*しな

branch, department

科 combines *rice* 禾 and *ladle for measuring* ⽃, suggesting the act of sorting rice into *different categories*.

Example sentences and meaning

1. **classify, classified thing**

* 彼は科学者です。
He is a scientist.
* 百科事典で調べてみよう。
I'll look it up in an encyclopedia.

2. **classification by species or type**

* 桜はバラ科の植物です。
The Japanese cherry belongs to the rose family.

Common compounds

理科系	りかけい	science major
文科系	ぶんかけい	liberal arts major
歯科医	しかい	dentist
内科	ないか	internal medicine
教科書	きょうかしょ	textbook

科 ↑↑ end strokes firmly

9 ノ 一 千 禾 禾 禾 科 科 科

科

---

171 海

カイ
うみ

sea, ocean

海 combines *water* ⺡, and *every, always* 毎, suggesting that water always returns to the *sea*.

Example sentences and meaning

1. **sea, ocean**

* 夏休みに海水浴をする
to swim in the sea during the summer holidays
* きれいな海だね。
The ocean is beautiful, isn't it?
* 海岸を散歩する
to walk along the seashore

2. **something wide and vast**

* 山は一面に火の海になった。
The whole mountain became engulfed in flames.

Common compounds

海外	かいがい	overseas, abroad
瀬戸内海	せとないかい	Inland Sea
*海女	あま	female pearl diver
*海苔	のり	edible seaweed, laver
*海老	えび	shrimp, prawn, lobster

海 stroke protrudes and ← ends with hook

9 ` ⼆ シ シ 氵 汇 海 海 海

海

---

172 活

カツ

*いき

life, activity

活 combines *water* 氵 and *tongue* 舌 to symbolize *life*.

Example sentences and meaning

1. lively, active

* あの人はとても活動的な人だ。
  He's a very active person.
* 人口が増えて町は活性化した。
  The population grew and injected new life into the town.

2. live, life

* 新しい生活に慣れてくる
  to become used to a lifestyle

3. save a person's life, revive

* 落ち込んでいた友人に活を入れる
  to cheer up a friend who feels depressed

Common compounds

活気	かっき	liveliness, vigor
活動	かつどう	activity
活火山	かっかざん	active volcano
活力	かつりょく	vitality, vigor
復活	ふっかつ	revival, resurrection

活 ← stroke sweeps down from right to left ヽ

9 ヽ ㇀ 氵 氵 汗 沃 活 活 活

活

Quiz 22 (167-172)

A. Write in kanji

1. tomorrow ___ ___
2. main entrance, front gate ___ ___
3. middle of the night ___ ___
4. internal medicine ___ ___
5. overseas, abroad ___ ___
6. lifestyle ___ ___
7. invention 発 ___
8. introductory book, handbook ___ 書

B. Write in hiragana

1. 深夜 _____
2. 教科書 _____
3. 瀬戸内海 _____
4. 活動的 _____
5. 説明書 _____
6. 門出 _____
7. 夜行列車 _____
8. 歯科医 _____
9. 海水浴 _____
10. 活火山 _____

C. Write in kanji

1. しょうめい 証 ___
2. もんかせい ___ ___ ___
3. びゃくや ___ ___
4. かがくしゃ ___ ___者
5. えび ___老
6. かつりょく ___ ___
7. ふめい 不 ___
8. ぶつもん 仏 ___

173 計

ケイ
はか・る、はか・らう
plan, measure, arrange

計 combines *say* 言 and *ten* 十 to suggest *measuring* in units of ten.

Example sentences and meaning

1. measure, count, investigate

* ちょっと計算してくれますか。
  Would you mind calculating this?
* 合計で三千六百六十円です。
  That totals to ¥3,660.

2. measuring device

* あの時計は五分遅れているみたい。
  That clock seems to be five minutes slow.
* 彼女は毎晩体重計にのっている。
  She weighs herself every evening.

3. contemplate, think about

* 夏休みの計画は？
  What are your plans for the summer vacation?

Common compounds

統計	とうけい	statistics
温度計	おんどけい	thermometer
生計	せいけい	livelihood, living
設計	せっけい	design, planning
小計	しょうけい	subtotal

this stroke longer than → those above and below it 計

9 一 二 十 キ 言 言 言 言 計

計

174 後

ゴ、コウ
のち、あと、うし・ろ、お
く・れる
after, behind, later, back, late

後 combines *advance* 彳, *little* 幺, and *foot* 夂, in reference to someone who is walking slowly, and thus falling *behind*.

Example sentences and meaning

1. behind, toward the rear

* 列の後ろに並んで下さい。
  Please go to the end of the line.
* 猫は後足にけがをした。
  The cat injured its hind paw.

2. later, afterward

* 後でまた電話します。
  I'll call you back later.
* 午後なら時間があります。
  I'll have time in the afternoon.

3. be late, lag behind

* 彼は和菓子好きでは人後に落ちない。
  He is second to none in his love for Japanese sweets.

Common compounds

後半	こうはん	latter half
後退	こうたい	retreat, back down
最後	さいご	the last, the end
後世	こうせい	later ages, posterity
後楽園	こうらくえん	Kōrakuen (place)

後 ← bottom portion not 又

9 ′ ク 彳 彳 彳 衿 後 後 後

後

175 思　シ　おも・う　think

思 combines *heart* 心 and *brain* 田 (although now written using the character for field), to give the idea of *thought*.

Example sentences and meaning

1. consider, think

* もう一度大学に行きたいと思います。
  I'd like to go back to university.
* ときどき亡くなった母のことを思い出す。
  Sometimes I reminisce about my late mother.
* 突然いい考えを思い付いた。
  I suddenly hit upon a good idea.

2. be good to a person

* 彼女は本当にお母さん思いの娘だ。
  She's a daughter who certainly takes good care of her mother.

Common compounds

思考	しこう	thinking, thought
思想	しそう	thought, idea
思い出	おもいで	memory, remembrance
思春期	ししゅんき	puberty, adolescence
不思議	ふしぎ	wonder, mystery, strangeness

思
↑ stroke ends with hook

9 丿 冂 冊 甲 田 甲 思 思 思

176 室　シツ　むろ　room

室 combines *arrow* 玄, *earth* 土, and *roof* 宀. The arrow hitting earth suggests arrive, so with roof, this came to mean a place to come to, i.e., a *room*.

Example sentences and meaning

1. room

* 室内では禁煙です。
  The indoor area is nonsmoking.
* 温室に入る
  to go into a greenhouse
* 603号室の鍵を下さい。
  Could I have the key to room 603, please.

2. a hole dug in the ground for storage

* これは昔、氷を貯蔵しておく氷室でした。
  This was once a room used to store ice.

3. house, family

* 昨年は皇室の行事がたくさんあった。
  Last year the Imperial Household held many social functions.

Common compounds

室外	しつがい	outdoor
教室	きょうしつ	classroom
暗室	あんしつ	darkroom
王室	おうしつ	royal family
寝室	しんしつ	bedroom

室
← this stroke longer than one above it

9 丶 宀 宀 宀 空 空 空 室 室

177 首

シュ
くび
head, neck, first

首 originally depicted a person's *head* with hair on top.

Example sentences and meaning

1. neck, head

* きりんは首が長い。
  Giraffes have long necks.

* テニスをして手首を痛めた。
  I hurt my wrist playing tennis.

2. the first, head, pivot

* 東京は日本の首都です。
  Tōkyō is the capital of Japan.

3. a counter for poems

* 百人一首をやったことある？
  Have you ever played the card game Hundred Poems By One Hundred Poets?

Common compounds

首輪	くびわ	necklace, collar
足首	あしくび	ankle
党首	とうしゅ	party leader
部首	ぶしゅ	kanji radical
首尾一貫	しゅびいっかん	consistency

首 ← top strokes slant inward

9 ` ` ` ` ナ 扩 首 首 首

178 秋

シュウ
あき
autumn, fall

秋 combines *rice plant* 禾 and *fire* 火, a reference to drying the rice stalks after the *fall* harvesting.

Example sentences and meaning

1. autumn, fall

* 秋が一番好きな季節です。
  Fall is my favorite season.

* 秋分の日はお休みです。
  Autumnal Equinox Day is a holiday.

2. years and months, time

* 彼と会える日を一日千秋の思いで待っていた。
  I waited impatiently for the day when I would be able to meet him.

Common compounds

秋分	しゅうぶん	autumnal equinox
秋晴れ	あきばれ	clear autumn weather
秋雨	あきさめ	autumn rain
秋田県	あきたけん	Akita Prefecture (place)
*秋刀魚	さんま	mackerel

秋 ← align bottom

9 ′ 二 千 千 禾 禾 利 秒 秋

Quiz 23 (173-178)

A. Write in English

1. 計算 _____
2. 最後 _____
3. 思春期 _____
4. 温室 _____
5. 党首 _____
6. 秋晴れ _____
7. 生計 _____
8. 後半 _____

C. Match the kanji with its reading

1. 温度計 ____   a. きょうしつ
2. 後楽園 ____   b. たいじゅうけい
3. 不思議 ____   c. おんどけい
4. 教室 ____   d. あとあし
5. 百人一首 ____   e. こうらくえん
6. 秋雨 ____   f. ふしぎ
7. 体重計 ____   g. あきさめ
8. 後足 ____   h. ひゃくにんいっしゅ

B. Write in kanji and kana

1. おもいだす   ___ ___ ___ ___
2. しつない   ___ ___
3. あしくび   ___ ___
4. しゅうぶんのひ   ___ ___ ___ ___
5. けいかく   ___ ___
6. れつのうしろ   列 ___ ___ ___
7. おもいで   ___ ___ ___
8. しんしつ   寝 ___
9. くびわ   ___輪
10. あきたけん   ___ ___ 県

---

179 春

シュン
はる
spring

春 combines *budding plant* 夆 and *sun* 日, a reference to *spring*.

Example sentences and meaning

1. spring

* 今日春一番が吹いた。
The first winds of spring blew today.

* 来春社会人になります。
I'll start my first full-time job this spring.

2. the beginning of the year

* 新春らしい明るい着物ですね。
That's a bright New Year's kimono.

3. sexual desire

* 子供が思春期を迎える年頃になった。
My children have reached puberty.

4. youth

* 青春時代は二度訪れない。
There's no reliving one's youth.

Common compounds

春分   しゅんぶん   vernal equinox
早春   そうしゅん   early spring
小春日和   こはるびより   balmy autumn weather, Indian summer
*春日   かすが   Kasuga (name)

this stroke longer → 春 ← stroke tapers off
than those above it

9   一 二 三 丰 夫 夫 表 春 春

春

180

食

ショク、*ジキ
た・べる、く・う
food, eating

食 derived from a pictograph of a tall vessel filled with *food* and covered by a lid.

Example sentences and meaning

1. eat, food

* 今晩何を食べようか。
  What shall we eat this evening?
* 食後に薬をのむ
  to take medicine after a meal

2. to bite, sting

* 蚊に食われてかゆい。
  I've been bitten by a mosquito and it's itchy.

3. figuratively, be consumed

* 今晩は月食が見られる。
  We can see a lunar eclipse tonight.

Common compounds

食事	しょくじ	meal, dining
食欲	しょくよく	appetite
定食	ていしょく	set course meal
腐食	ふしょく	corrosion
菜食主義者	さいしょくしゅぎしゃ	vegetarian

食 ← strokes connect

9 ノ 人 人 今 今 今 食 食 食

食

181

星

セイ、*ショウ
ほし
star

星 combines *sun, light* 日 and *seedling* 生, a reference to emerging light. This then took on the meaning of *star*.

Example sentences and meaning

1. star

* 今日は星がよく見える。
  The stars are very bright tonight.
* 北極星は動かないので目印になる。
  Since the North Star is stationary, it can be used as a guide.

2. guide, aim

* やっと契約できる目星がついた。
  It seems likely that we will finally be able to get the contract.

3. symbol of wins and losses

* 大関は星を落とした。
  The champion sumo wrestler lost his bout.

Common compounds

火星	かせい	Mars
惑星	わくせい	planet
彗星	すいせい	comet
図星	ずぼし	bull's eye
星占い	ほしうらない	astrology, horoscope

星 ← this stroke longer than those above it

9 丨 冂 冂 日 日 尸 早 早 星

星

182 前

ゼン
まえ

before, front

前 combines *boat* 月, *foot* ⌐ and *sword* 刂. From cutting off the rope and pushing off from shore comes the meaning *advance*, which evolved to *before*.

Example sentences and meaning

1. before, front

* 駅前にタクシー乗り場がある。
There is a taxi stand in front of the station.

2. the previous section

* 憲法の前文を読む
to read the preamble to the constitution

3. prior to a certain time

* その人とは前に会ったことがある。
I've met that person before.

4. portion

* ラーメンを二人前出前して下さい。
Could I have two bowls of ramen delivered, please?

Common compounds

午前	ごぜん	morning, A.M.
前半	ぜんはん	the first half
前列	ぜんれつ	front row
前髪	まえがみ	bangs
前橋	まえばし	Maebashi (place)

前　← stroke ends with hook

9　丷 丷 广 产 芢 肖 前 前

前

183 茶

チャ、サ

tea, light brown

茶 combines *plant* ⺾ and *ample* 余, suggesting one's ample, or relaxed feelings when drinking *tea*.

Example sentences and meaning

1. tea

* 紅茶にしますか。
Would you like some tea?

2. tea ceremony

* 昨日茶会に行った。
I went to a tea ceremony yesterday.

3. light brown

* 黒い髪を茶色に染める
to dye black hair a light brown color

4. something haphazard or unreasonable

* あまり焦って無茶をするなよ。
Don't be so impatient and reckless!

Common compounds

喫茶店	きっさてん	café
日本茶	にほんちゃ	Japanese (green) tea
茶室	ちゃしつ	tea-ceremony room
麦茶	むぎちゃ	barley tea
茶目	ちゃめ	prankster

茶　← bottom portion not 木

9　一 ⺊ ⺊ 犭 岁 岁 芐 茶 茶

茶

184 昼

チュウ
ひる

daytime, noon

昼 now consists of *measure* 尺, *sun* 日, and *one* 一, suggesting the most amount of sun is at *noon*.

Example sentences and meaning

1. **daytime, in the day**
   * 夏は昼が長い。
     The days are long in summer.
   * 昼間は仕事で忙しいのです。
     During the day I'm busy with work.

2. **noon, afternoon**
   * 昼食はまだですか。
     Isn't lunch ready yet?
   * お昼前に一仕事済ませよう。
     Let's get one job over and done with before noon.

Common compounds

白昼	はくちゅう	daytime, broad daylight
昼休み	ひるやすみ	lunch break
昼飯	ひるめし	lunch
昼夜	ちゅうや	day and night
真昼	まひる	broad daylight, midday

昼 ← does not touch 日

9 ｱ ｺ ｼ 尺 尺 尽 屄 屄 昼 昼

昼

Test 7 (161-184)

A. Write in kanji
1. しゅんぶん ___ ___
2. げっしょく ___ ___
3. かせい ___ ___
4. ぜんはん ___ ___
5. ちゃいろ ___ ___
6. ちゅうや ___ ___
7. ちょくご ___ ___
8. とうほく ___ ___
9. ごうけい ___ ___
10. ごご ___ ___

B. Write in kanji and kana
1. dawn ___ ___
2. sluice gate ___ ___
3. nocturnal ___ ___ 性
4. female pearl diver ___ ___
5. liveliness, vigor ___ ___
6. Kasuga ___ ___
7. after a meal ___ ___
8. two portions ___ ___ ___
9. prankster ___ ___
10. lunch break ___ ___ ___

C. Write in English
1. 冬の夜が長い。

2. レースの時間を計る

3. 直ちに時計を直して下さい。

4. 犬は店の後ろでえさを食べていた。

5. まだ明るいうちに歩いていきましょう。

6. 妹は門の前に立っていた。

7. 秋山さんは今年の春、首になった。

8. 星がかがやく秋の夜

9. 明日海へ行きたいと思っています。

10. あの科学者の家の後ろに茶室がある。

D. Fill in the kanji and translate
1. (＾かすが＾) くんは (＾なに＾) も (＾し＾) らないのが (＾あき＾) らかだ。

2. えきの (＾ひがしぐち＾) から (＾で＾) て、(時＾とけいだい＾) まで (＾ある＾) いて (＾くだ＾) さい。

3. お (＾ねえ＾) さんの (＾あか＾) いセーターの (＾くび＾) のところが (＾むし＾) に (＾く＾) われた。

4. マラソン (＾だいかい＾) でぼくはみんなに (＾ごひゃく＾) メートル (＾おく＾) れてゴールインした。ぼくの (＾うし＾) ろにはだれもいなかった。

5. (＾きょう＾) の (＾ごご＾) の (＾てんきよほう＾ 予報) ははれ (＾のち＾) くもりだった。

6. (＾ひる＾) も (＾よる＾) も (＾まえだ＾) くんはいつも (＾きょうかしょ＾ 教) ばっかりよんでいるね。

7. (＾もり＾) の (＾なか＾) にある (＾ちい＾) さな (＾いしむろ＾) の (＾ちか＾) くで (＾ひがし＾) さんと (＾ふたり＾) で (＾ちょうしょく＾) を (＾た＾) べた。

8. (＾あおもり＾) から (＾き＾) た (＾まえだ＾) くんにとっては (＾とうきょう＾) での (＾がっこうせいかつ＾) になれるのが (＾たいへん＾ 変) だった。

9. (＾たなか＾) さんの (＾いもうと＾) の (＾とし＾) は (＾し＾) っているけれども (＾なまえ＾) を (＾おもいだ＾) せない。

10. あの (＾とし＾)、(＾あき＾) の (＾ほしぞら＾) の (＾した＾) で (＾なが＾) いあいだあなたと (＾うみ＾) ぞいのみちを (＾ある＾) いたことを (＾いま＾) でもこいしく (＾おも＾) っている。

185

点　テン
point, dot

点 now combines *occupy* 占 and *fire* 灬, suggesting a *black mark* left by fire.

Example sentences and meaning

1. **point, dot**
   * 点と線
     point and line

2. **designated place, time**
   * 次は終点です。
     The next stop is the end of the line.
   * 要点を先に言う
     to give the main points first

3. **grade, mark for scoring**
   * あと一点で満点だったのに。
     One more and your score would have been perfect.

4. **counter for pieces of work, garments**
   * 写真を十五点選んだ。
     I selected 15 photographs.

Common compounds

得点	とくてん	score
点検	てんけん	inspection
点字	てんじ	Braille
欠点	けってん	defect, flaw
問題点	もんだいてん	the point in question

note way dots are drawn → 点

9　丶 ト ヤ 占 占 占 点 点 点

点

186

南　ナン、*ナ
みなみ
south

南 can be thought of as *ten* 十 houses with *plants* 半 growing *inside* 冂, a reference to villages in *southern* areas.

Example sentence and meaning

1. **south**
   * ペンギンはもともと南極の鳥です。
     Penguins are from the South Pole.
   * 沖縄は日本の南西地方です。
     Okinawa occupies the southwestern region of Japan.
   * 東南アジアの島でのんびり休暇を楽しむ
     to enjoy a holiday relaxing on an island in Southeast Asia

Common compounds

南下	なんか	go south
南風	みなみかぜ	south wind
南向き	みなみむき	facing south
南緯	なんい	south latitude
南北	なんぼく	north and south

bottom portion not 半→ 南　← stroke ends with hook

9　一 十 十 両 两 两 南 南 南

南

187 風

フウ、*フ
かぜ
wind, appearance, style

風 combines *sail* 几 and *insect* 虫, suggesting insects blown against a sail by the *wind*.

Example sentences and meaning

1. **wind**

* 夕べは何時間も強風が吹いていた。
There was a strong wind blowing for hours last night.

2. **custom**

* その地方には独特の風習がある。
That region has its distinctive customs.

3. **appearance, scene**

* イギリスの風景画が好きだ。
I'm fond of English landscape paintings.

* 日本の家は和風と洋風が混ざっている。
Japanese houses are a mixture of Japanese and Western styles.

Common compounds

台風	たいふう	typhoon
春風	はるかぜ	spring breeze
古風	こふう	old style, old custom
学風	がくふう	academic traditions
*風邪	かぜ	a cold

風 ← stroke ends with hook

9 | 丿 几 凡 凡 凨 凮 風 風 風

風

188 夏

カ、*ゲ
なつ
summer

夏 derived from a pictograph of a masked person dancing, perhaps in a *summer* festival.

Example sentences and meaning

1. **summer**

* 明日から学校は夏休みだ。
School summer vacation begins tomorrow.

* 夏バテして辛いなあ。
This summer heat has worn me out.

* 日本には夏時間はありません。
Japan has no daylight saving time.

* 常夏の島ハワイ
Hawaii, land of eternal summer

Common compounds

立夏	りっか	first day of summer
初夏	しょか	early summer
夏休み	なつやすみ	summer vacation
*夏至	げし	summer solstice

夏 ← bottom portion not 又

10 | 一 ア ア 百 百 百 頁 夏 夏

夏

189

家

カ、ケ
いえ、や
house

家 combines *roof* 宀 and *pig* 豕, suggesting a place where pigs and humans are together, i.e., a *house*.

Example sentences and meaning

1. house
* 台風で民家に被害が出た。
  Houses were damaged by the typhoon.
* 古い家具を直してまた使う
  to repair and reuse old furniture

2. family
* 私は家族と一緒に住んでいます。
  I live with my family.
* 家業を継ぐために田舎に帰ります。
  I'm returning to my hometown to take over the family business.

3. specialist
* 川端康成はノーベル賞作家でした。
  Yasunari Kawabata was a Nobel prize-winning author.

Common compounds

大家	おおや	landlord
家庭	かてい	home, family
専門家	せんもんか	specialist, expert
政治家	せいじか	politician

stroke ends with hook 家

10　丶丶宀宀宇宇宇家家家

家

190

記

キ
しる・す
write down, note

記 combines *words* 言 and *winding thread* 己, which can be thought of as tying words together in *writing*.

Example sentences and meaning

1. write down, note
* ここに名前と住所を記入して下さい。
  Please write your name and address here.
* この記号は何ですか。
  What does this symbol represent?

2. something written, document
* 新聞の記事を読む
  to read a newspaper article

3. remember
* あの人の名前は記憶していない。
  I don't remember that person's name.

Common compounds

記録	きろく	record
日記	にっき	diary, journal
速記	そっき	shorthand
記念	きねん	commemoration
明記	めいき	clearly state, specify

記 ← stroke ends with hook

10　丶亠亠言言言言記記記

記

Quiz 24 (185-190)

A. Write in kanji

1. さっか　　　＿＿ ＿＿
2. きにゅう　　＿＿ ＿＿
3. じゅうごてん　＿＿ ＿＿ ＿＿
4. なんぼく　　＿＿ ＿＿
5. はるかぜ　　＿＿ ＿＿
6. なつじかん　＿＿ 時間
7. おおや　　　＿＿ ＿＿
8. にっき　　　＿＿ ＿＿

B. Write in hiragana

1. 問題点　＿＿＿＿＿＿＿＿＿
2. 南極　＿＿＿＿＿＿＿＿＿
3. 強風　＿＿＿＿＿＿＿＿＿
4. 夏休み　＿＿＿＿＿＿＿＿＿
5. 専門家　＿＿＿＿＿＿＿＿＿
6. 記号　＿＿＿＿＿＿＿＿＿
7. 終点　＿＿＿＿＿＿＿＿＿
8. 西南地方　＿＿＿＿＿＿＿＿＿
9. 風習　＿＿＿＿＿＿＿＿＿
10. 初夏　＿＿＿＿＿＿＿＿＿

C. Write in English

1. 家具　＿＿＿＿＿＿＿＿＿
2. 明記　＿＿＿＿＿＿＿＿＿
3. 点字　＿＿＿＿＿＿＿＿＿
4. 南風　＿＿＿＿＿＿＿＿＿
5. 立夏　＿＿＿＿＿＿＿＿＿
6. 家族　＿＿＿＿＿＿＿＿＿
7. 記録　＿＿＿＿＿＿＿＿＿
8. 洋風　＿＿＿＿＿＿＿＿＿

191　帰

キ
かえ・る、かえ・す
return, send back

帰 combines *broom* 帚 and *foot* ⼅, and can be thought of as a place where sweeping is done, i.e., the *home*. Home is an associated meaning of *return*.

Example sentences and meaning

1. return

* 雨が降りそうだから早く帰ろう。
Let's hurry home because it looks like it's going to rain.
* ご帰国はいつですか。
When do you return to your home country?

2. consequence, ultimate result

* 二人の意見は同じところへ帰結した。
Eventually they both came to the same conclusion.

3. conform, follow

* 彼はアメリカ人だったが日本に帰化した。
He changed his citizenship from American to Japanese.

Common compounds

帰宅	きたく	return, come home
復帰	ふっき	return, comeback
帰省	きせい	returning to one's hometown
帰京	ききょう	to return to Tōkyō
帰属	きぞく	revert to, return to

帰 ← stroke doesn't protrude
← stroke ends with hook

10 ｜ ⼅ ⼖ ⼶ ⼧ ⼨ ⼫ 帰 帰 帰

139

192 原

ゲン
はら

original, field, plain

原 combines *cliff* 厂 and *spring* 泉, suggesting the *origin* of a stream and the edge of a *field*.

Example sentences and meaning

1. **plain, flat, spacious area**
* 原っぱで昼寝をした。
I took a nap in an open field.

2. **origin, source**
* 原因と結果
cause and effect
* 原油の値上がりで物価が上がった。
Because of the rise in price of crude oil, commodity prices rose.
* カタログの宝石は原寸大です。
The gems in the catalogue are shown in actual size.

Common compounds

原料	げんりょう	raw materials
原稿	げんこう	manuscript
原形	げんけい	original form
河原	かわら	dry river bed
原子爆弾	げんしばくだん	atom bomb

原 ← middle stroke ends with hook

10 一 厂 厂 尺 斤 戶 盾 原 原 原

原

193 高

コウ
たか・い、たか・める

high, increase, raise

高 depicts a *high* lookout.

Example sentences and meaning

1. **high, advanced**
* このビルは日本一高いビルです。
This building is the tallest in Japan.
* いい車だけど高すぎるなあ。
It's a good car, but it's too expensive.

2. **be proud**
* あの人はいつも高圧的な態度をとる。
He is always very overbearing.

3. **an amount**
* 口座の残高を教えて下さい。
Please tell me the balance of my account.

4. **abbreviation of 高等学校 (senior high school)**
* 電車の中で女子高生が騒いでいた。
Some senior high school girls were making a lot of noise in the train.

Common compounds

高価	こうか	high price
高級	こうきゅう	high-grade, class, rank
高熱	こうねつ	high fever
最高	さいこう	maximum, best, great
売上高	うりあげだか	sales, amount sold

the 口 above larger → than the one below 高 ← stroke ends with hook

10 ` ㇒ 亠 亠 方 古 言 高 高 高 高

高

194 紙
シ
かみ
paper

紙 combines *threads* 糸 and *ladle* 氏, and can be thought of as stirring boiled threads to make *paper*.

Example sentences and meaning

1. paper

* コピー用紙、ある？
  Do you have any photocopy paper?
* 折り紙を折る
  to fold origami

2. newspaper

* 業界紙を読む
  to read a trade journal
* 会社では五紙取っている。
  We subscribe to five newspapers at our company.

Common compounds

和紙	わし	Japanese paper
紙幣	しへい	paper money
方眼紙	ほうがんし	graph paper
包装紙	ほうそうし	wrapping paper
手紙	てがみ	letter

紙　← stroke ends with hook

10 ｜ 乙 幺 幺 糸 弁 糸 糸 紅 紅 紙

紙

195 時
ジ
とき
time, hour

時 combines *sun* 日 and *temple* 寺, a place where people kept track of *time*.

Example sentences and meaning

1. time, hour

* ちょっとお時間ありますか。
  Do you have a moment?
* いらいらして何度も時計を見た。
  He kept glancing impatiently at his watch.
* 北京と東京の時差は何時間ですか。
  How many hours' time difference is there between Beijing and Tōkyō?

2. of a particular time

* 当時を知る人はおじいさんだけです。
  Only grandfather knows what life was like then.

3. occasionally

* 時々夕食を作る
  to sometimes make dinner

Common compounds

時々	ときどき	sometimes
時給	じきゅう	payment by the hour
時速	じそく	speed per hour
時価	じか	current price
七時間	しちじかん	seven hours

時　← stroke ends with hook

10 ｜ 丨 冂 刀 日 旺 旷 旷 時 時

時

196 弱　ジャク
よわ・い、よわ・まる
weak

弱 originally depicted two fledgling birds side by side, thus giving the idea of *weak*.

Example sentences and meaning

1. weak, lacking energy

* やっと雨足が弱まった。
  Finally this pouring rain has lightened up.
* 彼は気が弱くて、友達ができない。
  He's so timid he's unable to make friends.

2. weak, poor at

* 母は機械に弱い。
  My mother isn't mechanically minded.

3. slightly less

* 駅までバスで一時間弱かかった。
  It took a little less than an hour to get to the station by bus.

Common compounds

弱虫	よわむし	weakling, coward
弱点	じゃくてん	weak point, a weakness
弱冠	じゃっかん	twenty years old, youth
病弱	びょうじゃく	delicate constitution
強弱	きょうじゃく	(relative) strength

弱　strokes end with hook

10　一　フ　弓　弓　弓　弓　弓　弱　弱　弱

弱

Quiz 25 (191-196)

A. Write in hiragana

1. 復帰 _____
2. 原因 _____
3. 高級 _____
4. 包装紙 _____
5. 時価 _____
6. 一時間弱 _____
7. 帰京 _____
8. 原料 _____

B. Write in English

1. 高熱 _____
2. コピー用紙 _____
3. 時速 _____
4. 弱点 _____
5. 帰宅 _____
6. 原子爆弾 _____
7. 最高 _____
8. 業界紙 _____
9. 時差 _____
10. 病弱 _____

C. Write in kanji

1. きこく _____
2. げんゆ ___油
3. うりあげだか ___ ___ ___
4. てがみ ___ ___
5. とけい ___ ___
6. よわむし ___ ___
7. ときどき ___々
8. げんすんだい ___寸___

197 書

ショ
か・く
write, writing

書 combines *hand holding a brush* 聿 and *thing* 曰 (a simple form of 者), to suggest *writing* something with a brush.

Example sentences and meaning

1. write

* カタカナで名前を書いて下さい。
Please write your name in katakana.

2. penmanship, writing style

* 書道の先生
master of Japanese calligraphy

3. letter, book, documents

* 一緒に書店に行こうか。
Let's go to the bookshop.

* 申込書を書く
to write an application

Common compounds

書道	しょどう	oriental calligraphy
書類	しょるい	documents
辞書	じしょ	dictionary
書斎	しょさい	study room
申込書	もうしこみしょ	application form

書 ← this stroke longer than those above and below

10 ｜ フ ユ ヨ ヨ 圭 聿 書 書 書

書

---

198 通

ツウ
とお・る、かよ・う
go through, pass, commute

通 combines *go* ⻌ and *fence* 甬 to give the meaning of *pass through*.

Example sentences and meaning

1. commute, go to and from

* 通勤電車の混み方はひどい。
The crowds on the commuter trains are horrible!

2. go, pass through

* 目白通りを通って下さい。
Please go along Mejiro Avenue.

3. well-informed person, inform, guide

* 彼は音楽通です。
He has a thorough knowledge of music.

4. a counter for documents, letters

* 最近手紙が一通も来ない。
I haven't received a single letter lately.

Common compounds

交通	こうつう	traffic, transport
通過	つうか	pass by/through
通訳	つうやく	interpreting, interpreter
夜通し	よどおし	all night long
一方通行	いっぽうつうこう	one-way traffic

通 ← stroke ends with hook

10 ｜ フ マ ア 丙 丙 甬 甬 涌 通 通

通

199 馬
バ
うま、*ま
horse

馬 derived from a pictograph of a *horse*, showing it's four legs and a tail drooping downwards.

Example sentences and meaning

1. **horse**
   * 最近乗馬をはじめました。
     I recently took up horse-riding.
   * 女性にも競馬は人気がある。
     Horse racing is popular with women as well.
   * 馬の耳に念仏
     Preaching to deaf ears (*lit.* A sutra in a horse's ear)

Common compounds

馬車	ばしゃ	horse-drawn carriage
木馬	もくば	rocking horse, vaulting horse
馬力	ばりき	horsepower
竹馬	たけうま, ちくば	stilts

馬 ← stroke ends with hook

10 丨 厂 厂 厈 厈 馬 馬 馬 馬 馬

馬

200 魚
ギョ
うお、さかな
fish

魚 derived from a pictograph of a *fish* on its side, mouth pointing upwards.

Example sentences and meaning

1. **fish**
   * 刺身もいいけど、焼き魚も好きだ。
     Raw fish is fine, but I like grilled fish, too.
   * 近所の魚屋でまぐろを買う
     to buy tuna at a local fish shop
   * 金魚を五匹飼っています。
     I have five goldfish.
   * 魚偏の漢字はたくさんある。
     There are many Chinese characters with the *sakana* radical.

Common compounds

魚市場	うおいちば	fish market
鮮魚	せんぎょ	fresh fish
魚介類	ぎょかいるい	fish and shellfish
熱帯魚	ねったいぎょ	tropical fish
淡水魚	たんすいぎょ	freshwater fish

note there are four dots → 魚

11 丿 勹 勹 勽 甪 甪 甶 鱼 魚 魚 魚

魚

201 強

キョウ、ゴウ
つよ・い、つよ・める、し・いる

strong

強 combines *bow* 弓 which represents *strength,* and 虫, which originally meant horsefly, a *strong,* persistent bug.

Example sentences and meaning

1. strong

* 彼は腕の力が強い。
  He has powerful arms.

2. one's strong point

* 彼は数学に強い。
  He's good at mathematics.

3. force, compel

* 強引にお酒を飲まされた。
  They forced me to drink alcohol.

4. a little more than

* その荷物は十キロ強ある。
  That baggage weighs a little over ten kilograms.

Common compounds

強固	きょうこ	firm, solid
強国	きょうこく	strong country, great power
勉強	べんきょう	study
強制	きょうせい	compulsory, forced
強調	きょうちょう	emphasis, stress

one stroke → 強

11 　フ　ユ　弓　弓'　弘'　弘'　弘''　強　強　強

強

202 教

キョウ
おし・える、おそ・わる

teach, religion

教 combines *stick* 攵, *adult* 耂, and *child* 子, to represent a person holding a stick and *teaching* a child.

Example sentences and meaning

1. teach, be taught

* 子供の頃ピアノを教わっていた。
  I was taught piano as a child.

* 教科書と辞典を買う
  to buy a textbook and a dictionary

2. inform

* 電話番号を教えて。
  Could you tell me your telephone number?

3. religion, learning

* 毎週日曜日には教会へ行きます。
  I go to church every Sunday.

* 一応仏教徒です。
  Technically I'm Buddhist.

Common compounds

教科	きょうか	subject, curriculum
教師	きょうし	instructor, teacher
教授	きょうじゅ	professor
宗教	しゅうきょう	religion
キリスト教	きりすときょう	Christianity

stroke ends with hook → 教

11 　一　十　土　耂　耂　考　考　孝　教　教　教

教

Quiz 26 (197-202)

A. Write in kanji

1. しょどう　　　　　　＿＿道
2. いっぽうつうこう　　＿＿ ＿＿ ＿＿

　　　　　　　　　　　＿＿
3. ばしゃ　　　　　　　＿＿
4. さかなや　　　　　　＿＿屋
5. きょうこく　　　　　＿＿ ＿＿
6. きょうかしょ　　　　＿＿ ＿＿ ＿＿
7. しょてん　　　　　　＿＿ ＿＿
8. よどおし　　　　　　＿＿ ＿＿

B. Match the kanji with its English meaning

1. application form	＿＿	a.	熱帯魚
2. interpreting	＿＿	b.	勉強
3. horsepower	＿＿	c.	乗馬
4. tropical fish	＿＿	d.	申込書
5. force	＿＿	e.	魚市場
6. religion	＿＿	f.	馬力
7. horse-riding	＿＿	g.	教会
8. fish market	＿＿	h.	宗教
9. study	＿＿	i.	通訳
10. church	＿＿	j.	強引

C. Write in hiragana

1. 辞書　　＿＿＿＿＿＿＿＿
2. 交通　　＿＿＿＿＿＿＿＿
3. 竹馬　　＿＿＿＿＿＿＿＿
4. 金魚　　＿＿＿＿＿＿＿＿
5. 強調　　＿＿＿＿＿＿＿＿
6. 教師　　＿＿＿＿＿＿＿＿
7. 通知　　＿＿＿＿＿＿＿＿
8. 焼き魚　＿＿＿＿＿＿＿＿

203　黄　オウ、コウ
　　　　き、*こ
　　　　yellow

黄 derived from a pictograph of a burning oil-tipped arrow, whose flames were *yellow*.

Example sentences and meaning

1. **yellow**

* 青と黄色の絵の具を混ぜる
  to mix blue and yellow paints
* 卵の黄身と白身を分ける
  to separate the egg yolk from the white
* 白いTシャツが黄ばんできた。
  My white T-shirt has yellowed.
* ツタンカーメンの黄金のマスク
  King Tut's golden mask

Common compounds

黄葉	こうよう	golden autumn leaves
黄砂	こうさ	yellow sand
*硫黄	いおう	sulphur
*黄金色	こがねいろ	golden color

center vertical stroke touches above line → 黄

11　一 十 卄 芢 芢 芑 芇 芇 莤 黄 黄

黄

204 黒

コク
くろ、くろ・い
black

黒 combines *field* 田, *soil* 土, and *fire* 灬 to suggest the *black* color of a burnt field.

Example sentences and meaning

1. black

* 白黒の写真を撮る
  to take black-and-white photographs
* 掃除したら手が真っ黒になった。
  My hands became filthy when I cleaned it.

2. evil, be defeated

* あいつは腹黒い奴で、信用できないよ。
  That guy's malicious. He can't be trusted!
* 事件の黒幕は彼だと言われている。
  He is the one who is said to have masterminded the incident.

Common compounds

黒字	くろじ	in the black
黒潮	くろしお	the Japan Current
暗黒	あんこく	darkness
黒人	こくじん	a black person
黒子	*ほくろ	mole (facial)

longer → 黒 ← longest

11　丨 冂 冂 日 甲 甲 里 里 黒 黒 黒

205 細

サイ
ほそ・い、ほそ・る、こま・かい
thin, detailed

細 combines *thread* 糸 and *field* 田 and can be thought of as partitioning a field into narrow sections.

Example sentences and meaning

1. thin, weak

* ボタンをつけるにはこの糸は細すぎる。
  This thread is too fine to sew a button.
* 彼女は細い声で返事をした。
  She replied in a feeble voice.

2. small shape/amount

* たまねぎを細かくきざんで
  dice the onions
* そんな細かいこと、どうでもいいよ。
  Why bother about such trivial details?

3. detailed

* 見積もりの明細書をくれますか。
  Could you give me an estimate with the details clearly listed, please?

Common compounds

詳細	しょうさい	details, particulars
繊細	せんさい	delicate, fine, subtle
細胞	さいぼう	cell (biological)
細工	さいく	workmanship, trick
細川	ほそかわ	Hosokawa (name)

糸 slightly taller at both ends than 田 → 細

11　乙 幺 幺 糸 糸 糸 糸 細 細 細

206 週　シュウ
week

週 originally meant *going* 辶 around a *field* 周; i.e., making a circuit. This came to mean *cycle of time,* and then *week.*

Example sentences and meaning

1. week

* 一週間はすぐ経ってしまう。
  A week passes in no time.
* 週刊誌を電車の中で読む
  to read a weekly magazine in the train
* この会社は週休二日です。
  This company has a five-day working week.
* 週末には何をするつもりですか。
  Do you have any plans for the weekend?
* 来週はちょっと忙しいですね。
  I'll be a little busy next week.

Common compounds

隔週	かくしゅう	every other week
週日	しゅうじつ	weekday
毎週	まいしゅう	every week, weekly
先週	せんしゅう	last week
週給	しゅうきゅう	weekly pay

週 ← stroke ends with hook

11　丿 冂 月 月 尸 用 周 周 周 调 週

週

---

207 雪　セツ　ゆき
snow

雪 combines *rain* 雨 and *broom* ヨ, suggesting that the rain is really *snow.*

Example sentences and meaning

1. snow

* 雪が降って一面真っ白だ。
  It snowed and blanketed everything in white.
* 春先には雪崩が多い。
  There are frequent avalanches in early spring.
* 積雪が三メートルある。
  The snow is three meters deep.

2. vindicate oneself

* 第一試合では惨敗だったが第二試合で雪辱を果たした。
  We lost our first match badly, but we redeemed ourselves by winning our second match.

Common compounds

除雪	じょせつ	snow removal
粉雪	こなゆき	powder snow
雪解け	ゆきどけ	thaw
雪だるま	ゆきだるま	snowman
*吹雪	ふぶき	blizzard, snowstorm

雪 ← center stroke doesn't protrude

11　一 广 广 雨 雨 雨 雨 雪 雪 雪

雪

208 船	セン ふね、*ふな ship	船 combines 舟 *(boat)* and 㕣 *(flowing water in ravine),* suggesting a large *boat* capable of going against a current.

Example sentences and meaning

1. ship

* 祖父は船で英国へ行った。
My grandfather went to England by ship.

* 港は船出を見送る人でいっぱいだった。
The harbor was full of people seeing off the ship.

* 船便で荷物が届いた。
A parcel arrived by surface mail.

* ここは造船業で栄えた町です。
This town has prospered due to the shipbuilding industry.

Common compounds

漁船	ぎょせん	fishing boat
風船	ふうせん	balloon
貨物船	かもつせん	freighter
飛行船	ひこうせん	airship, blimp
船橋	ふなばし	Funabashi (place)

stroke goes up from → 船
left to the right

11	′	⺁	凢	月	舟	舟′	舟ヽ	船ヽ	船	船

| 船 | | | | | | | | | | |

Test 8

Test 8 (161-208)

A. Write in kanji and kana

1. おうごん ___ ___
2. こくじん ___ ___
3. ほそかわ ___ ___
4. まいしゅう ___ ___
5. ゆきだるま ___ ___ ___ ___
6. ふなで ___ ___
7. きいろ ___ ___
8. しろくろ ___ ___
9. さいく ___ ___
10. しゅうじつ ___ ___
11. なんきょく ___ 極
12. たいふう ___ ___
13. めじろどおり ___ ___
14. もくば ___ ___ ___
15. きょうかい ___ ___

B. Write in English

1. 雪解け ___
2. 船便 ___
3. 黄葉 ___
4. 真っ黒 ___
5. 明細書 ___
6. 週刊誌 ___
7. 漁船 ___
8. 吹雪 ___
9. 時計 ___
10. 後足 ___
11. 思考 ___
12. 王室 ___
13. 首都 ___
14. 家族 ___
15. 満点 ___

C. Write in hiragana

1. 黄身 ___
2. 黒字 ___
3. 詳細 ___
4. 週給 ___
5. 雪崩 ___
6. 風船 ___
7. 帰省 ___
8. 河原 ___
9. 高価 ___
10. 和紙 ___
11. 当時 ___
12. 強弱 ___

13. 書類 ___
14. 通過 ___
15. 風邪 ___

D. Match the the kanji with its reading

1. 黄金色 ___ a. ふなばし
2. 暗黒 ___ b. きょうか
3. 細胞 ___ c. こがねいろ
4. 週末 ___ d. かもつせん
5. 粉雪 ___ e. しゅうまつ
6. 船橋 ___ f. やきざかな
7. 九週間 ___ g. あんこく
8. 競馬 ___ h. きゅうしゅうかん
9. 焼き魚 ___ i. かてい
10. 強制 ___ j. けいば
11. 教科 ___ k. さいぼう
12. 家庭 ___ l. せんしゅう
13. 記事 ___ m. こなゆき
14. 先週 ___ n. きじ
15. 貨物船 ___ o. きょうせい

E. Write in English

1. 風が南からふいてくると気おんが上がる。

   ___

2. 父の体がだんだん弱くなてきた。

   ___

3. 白い紙に大きな字を書く

   ___

4. 今年の夏休みに書道を母に教わった。

   ___

5. 魚市場はどこにあるか教えて下さい。

   ___

6. 自分の家の前で力の強そうな男の人が雪かきをしていた。

   ___

7. 二人はあさ歩いて学校に通う。

   ___

8. あのせが高い女の子は足が弱いので、すぐつかれてしまう。

   ___

9. 外国で高まっている日本語ねつ

   ___

10. 自分の弱点もちゃんと考えてみて。

F. Fill in the kanji and translate

1. （<ruby>こんしゅう</ruby>）の（<ruby>かようび</ruby>　曜）に（<ruby>さかな</ruby>）をくわえ
   たねこが（<ruby>いえ</ruby>）の（<ruby>まえ</ruby>）を（<ruby>とお</ruby>）った。

2. この（<ruby>きいろ</ruby>）い（<ruby>かみ</ruby>）に（<ruby>なまえ</ruby>）を
   （<ruby>しる</ruby>）しなさい。

3. （<ruby>できごと</ruby>　事）の（<ruby>こま</ruby>）かい（<ruby>はなし</ruby>）は（<ruby>あと</ruby>）
   にしよう。

4. お（<ruby>ねえ</ruby>）さんがガスの（<ruby>ひ</ruby>）を（<ruby>つよ</ruby>）め
   たら、（<ruby>さかな</ruby>）が（真　<ruby>まっくろ</ruby>）にこげた。

5. あの（<ruby>こ</ruby>）は（<ruby>あし</ruby>）が（<ruby>ほそ</ruby>）くて、
   （<ruby>いろじろ</ruby>）で、うらやましい。

6. （<ruby>あに</ruby>）は（<ruby>じぶん</ruby>）の（<ruby>かんが</ruby>）えを（<ruby>ゆうじん</ruby>）
   に（<ruby>し</ruby>）いた。

7. （<ruby>ちち</ruby>）は（<ruby>こども</ruby>）の（<ruby>とき</ruby>）、（<ruby>べいこく</ruby>）
   から（<ruby>ちゅうごく</ruby>）へ（<ruby>ふね</ruby>）で（<ruby>い</ruby>）った。

8. （<ruby>たいふう</ruby>）の（<ruby>かぜ</ruby>）がまた（<ruby>つよ</ruby>）まるとい
   うので、（<ruby>がっこう</ruby>）は（<ruby>がくせい</ruby>）を（<ruby>かえ</ruby>）し
   た。

9. （<ruby>ときどき</ruby>　々）、（<ruby>いえ</ruby>）に（<ruby>かえ</ruby>）ってきてか
   ら、（<ruby>にっき</ruby>）をつけるのをわすれてしま
   う。

10. （<ruby>こども</ruby>）たちは（<ruby>はら</ruby>）っぱを
    （<ruby>はじ まわ</ruby>）っている（<ruby>くろ</ruby>）い（<ruby>うま</ruby>）を
    （<ruby>み</ruby>）ていた。

209 組

ソ
くみ、く・む
put together, class

組 combines *threads* 糸 and *piled up* 且, perhaps suggesting threads intertwined, which led to the meaning of *put together*.

Example sentences and meaning

1. put together, assemble

* ここはテープレコーダーの組み立て工場です。
  This is an assembly plant for tape recorders.

2. group, party

* 労働組合が二十四時間ストをしている。
  The labor union is holding a 24-hour strike.

* 彼とは同じ組でした。
  He and I were in the same class.

* 日本で一番大きな暴力団は山口組である。
  The largest criminal organization in Japan is the Yamaguchi-gumi.

Common compounds

組閣	そかく	formation of a cabinet
組み紐	くみひも	braided string
組曲	くみきょく	suite (music)
番組	ばんぐみ	program
骨組み	ほねぐみ	skeleton, framework

組 ⊊ same spacing

11 ﹄ ⼅ ⼂ 糸 糸 糸 糸 糸 紀 細 組

組

210 鳥

チョウ
とり
bird

鳥 evolved from a pictograph of a *bird* with a long tail drooping down.

Example sentences and meaning

1. bird

* シベリアから日本へ白鳥が渡ってきます。
  Swans migrate from Siberia to Japan.

* 寒くて鳥肌が立っている。
  I've got goose bumps from the cold.

* 子供のとき小鳥を飼いたくてしようがなかった。
  As a child I desperately wanted to have a small bird as a pet.

Common compounds

渡り鳥	わたりどり	migratory bird
水鳥	みずどり	waterfowl, aquatic bird
鳥かご	とりかご	bird cage
焼鳥	やきとり	grilled skewered chicken
七面鳥	しちめんちょう	turkey

鳥 ← this stroke longer than ones above and below it

11 ′ ⼂ ⼍ ⼍ 阜 阜 鳥 鳥 鳥 鳥 鳥

鳥

211 野

ヤ
の
field, wild

野 combines *village* 里 and *loose* 予, suggesting a spacious *rural* community.

Example sentences and meaning

1. **field, plain**
   * 野菜をもっと食べた方がいいよ。
   You'd better eat more vegetables.

2. **an expanse, extent**
   * 様々な分野の人が参加した。
   People from various fields attended.

3. **in a natural state**
   * 山には野生のサルが住んでいる。
   Wild monkeys live in the mountains.

4. **uncivilized, unrefined**
   * どうもあの人は粗野で困るね。
   There's something vulgar about that man that bothers me.

Common compounds

平野	へいや	a plain, open field
野宿	のじゅく	camping out
野球	やきゅう	baseball
野党	やとう	opposition party
上野	うえの	Ueno (place)

stroke goes up from left to right→ 野 ← stroke ends with hook

11 ｜ 冂 冃 日 甲 甲 里 野 野 野 野

野

212 理

リ
reason, truth, principle

理 combines *jewel* 王 and *village* 里, which acts phonetically to express split. From cutting a jewel came the meaning of *acting carefully,* and then *reason.*

Example sentences and meaning

1. **do methodically, arrange**
   * 料理がお上手ですね。
   You're a good cook.
   * 靴のかかとを修理しないとだめだ。
   I need the heel of my shoe repaired.
   * ビザの申請をてきぱきと処理してくれた。
   They promptly processed my visa application.

2. **reason, logic**
   * アインシュタインの相対性理論
   Einstein's Theory of Relativity

3. **natural science**
   * 大学の理系の学部に進むつもりです。
   I intend to study at the science department at the university.

Common compounds

理解	りかい	understand, comprehend
理由	りゆう	reason, cause
真理	しんり	truth
義理	ぎり	duty, honor
総理大臣	そうりだいじん	prime minister

stroke goes up from left to right → 理

11 一 T 千 王 王 玑 玗 玾 理 理 理

理

213 雲

ウン
くも
cloud

雲 combines *rain* 雨 and *billowing* 〓 to represent *clouds*.

Example sentences and meaning

1. cloud

* 雨雲が出てきた。
  Rain clouds have appeared.

2. something as numerous as clouds

* 天体望遠鏡でアンドロメダ星雲を見る
  to observe the Andromeda Nebula using a telescope

Common compounds

雲行き	くもゆき	cloud movement
雲集	うんしゅう	throng, crown, swarm
雲間	くもま	break between clouds
積乱雲	せきらんうん	cumulonimbus clouds
*雲脂	ふけ	dandruff

雲 ← this stroke longer than one above it

12	一 广 广 卉 雨 雨 雨 雨 雫 雲 雲 雲
雲	

214 絵

カイ、エ
picture

絵 combines *thread* 糸 and *meet* 会 to suggest an embroidered *picture*.

Example sentences and meaning

1. picture

* 子供の頃から絵を描くのが好きだ。
  I've liked drawing since my childhood.
* 趣味で油絵を描く
  to do oil painting as a hobby
* 印象派の絵画展を見に行く
  to go see an exhibition of Impressionist paintings
* 浮世絵は木版画です。
  Ukiyoe pictures are woodblock prints.

Common compounds

似顔絵	にがおえ	portrait, likeness
挿絵	さしえ	illustration (in a book)
絵の具	えのぐ	paints
絵葉書	えはがき	picture postcard
絵筆	えふで	paintbrush

絵 ← end stroke firmly

12	乡 乡 幺 纟 牟 糸 糸 糸 絵 絵 絵
絵	

Quiz 27 (209-214)

A. Write in English

1. 番組 _____
2. 七面鳥 _____
3. 分野 _____
4. 料理 _____
5. 雨雲 _____
6. 絵画展 _____
7. 組曲 _____
8. 白鳥 _____

B. Write in kanji

1. うえの _____ _____
2. りゆう _____ 由
3. くもゆき _____ _____
4. えふで _____ 筆
5. くみたて _____ _____
6. ことり _____ _____
7. へいや 平 _____
8. りかい _____ 解
9. くもま _____ 間
10. えはがき _____ 葉 _____

C. Match the kanji with its reading

1. 労働組合 _____   a. しゅうり
2. 渡り鳥 _____   b. えのぐ
3. 野球 _____   c. ろうどうくみあい
4. 修理 _____   d. やさい
5. 積乱雲 _____   e. わたりどり
6. 絵の具 _____   f. やきとり
7. 焼鳥 _____   g. せきらんうん
8. 野菜 _____   h. やきゅう

215

間

カン、ケン
あいだ、ま
interval, room, pause

間 combines *gate* 門 and *sun* 日, to indicate light shining through a space between the *gates*.

Example sentences and meaning

1. interval of time or space

* 滞在期間を延長する
  to extend the period of one's stay
* 間に合いましたか。
  Did you make it in time?
* 時間がたつのは速いね。
  Time flies, doesn't it?
* 会社は神田と銀座の中間にあります。
  The company is located midway between Kanda and Ginza Station.

2. a room, a counter for rooms

* 居間でテレビを見る
  to watch television in the living room

Common compounds

間接	かんせつ	indirect
空間	くうかん	space, the infinite
人間	にんげん	human being
昼間	ひるま	daytime
一週間	いっしゅうかん	a week

end stroke firmly → 間 ← stroke ends with hook

12 丨 冂 冂 冃 門 門 門 門 閈 間 間 間

間

216 場

ジョウ
ば
place

場 depicts the *sun* 日 *shining down* 勿 on the *ground* 土; perhaps suggesting a *place* in the sun.

Example sentences and meaning

1. **place**
   * 工場の場所を教えて下さい。
   Please tell me where the factory is.
   * コンサートの開場は六時です。
   The doors for the concert open at 6:00.

2. **time, occasion**
   * 雨の場合は試合は中止になる。
   If it rains, the game will be called off.
   * この言葉はどんな場面で使われますか。
   What kind of situation is this word used in?

3. **scene in a play**
   * 二幕八場の芝居
   a play in two acts and eight scenes

Common compounds

立場	たちば	standpoint, position
牧場	ぼくじょう	pasture, ranch, meadow
登場	とうじょう	appear on the scene
戦場	せんじょう	battlefield
競馬場	けいばじょう	race track

stroke goes up from left to right → 場 ← stroke ends with hook

12 一 十 土 圵 圹 坍 坦 坦 堨 場 場 場

場

217 晴

セイ
は・れる、は・らす
clear up, dispel

晴 combines *sun* 日 and *blue* 青 to suggest *clear weather*.

Example sentences and meaning

1. **fair weather**
   * 午後には晴れ間がのぞくでしょう。
   We may expect periods of clear weather in the afternoon.
   * 明日もきっと晴れだよ。
   I'm sure the weather will be fine tomorrow too!

2. **be cleared**
   * 彼は疑いが晴れた。
   He was cleared of all suspicion.

3. **in public**
   * 結婚式には晴れ着を着ます。
   I'll wear my best clothes to the wedding.

Common compounds

晴天	せいてん	clear weather
晴雨計	せいうけい	barometer
秋晴れ	あきばれ	fine autumn weather
晴れ晴れ	はればれ	cloudless, bright, cheerful

晴 ← stroke ends with hook

12 丨 冂 日 日 旦 日 旪 晴 晴 晴 晴 晴

晴

218 朝

チョウ
あさ
morning, dynasty

朝 shows the *sun rising behind plants* 卓 and the *moon* 月, which perhaps is being displaced by the *morning* sun.

Example sentences and meaning

1. morning

* ハイキングの日は早朝に家を出ます。
On days when I go hiking, I leave home early in the morning.

* 高山の朝市は有名です。
The morning market in Takayama is famous.

* 朝刊はまだ来てないよ。
The morning paper hasn't arrived yet.

2. dynasty

* 美しい絵巻物は平安朝文化の粋です。
Beautiful picture scrolls represent the quintessence of the culture of the Heian period.

Common compounds

早朝	そうちょう	early morning
朝ご飯	あさごはん	breakfast
毎朝	まいあさ	every morning
朝廷	ちょうてい	imperial court
*今朝	けさ	this morning

this stroke longer than those above it → 朝 ← stroke ends with hook

12 一 十 十 古 古 古 直 卓 卓 朝 朝 朝

朝

---

219 答

トウ
こた・える、こた・え
answer

答 combines *bamboo* 竹 and *fit, match* 合, which suggests that a bamboo cover that exactly matches its container is similar to a statement that directly answers a question.

Example sentences and meaning

1. answer

* 試験の答えがわからない。
I don't know the answers to the exam questions.

* 彼は質問を答えなかった。
He didn't answer the question.

* 講演の後で質疑応答の時間を設けます。
A question period will be held after the lecture.

* ファックスで問い合わせたが返答がない。
I made inquiries by fax, but there has been no response.

Common compounds

解答	かいとう	answer, solution
回答	かいとう	reply
即答	そくとう	prompt reply
答礼	とうれい	to return courtesy, salute
口答え	くちごたえ	talk back, retort

→ 答 ← nothing touches the 人

12 ノ ト ケ ゲ ゲ ゲ ゲ 竹 竺 芡 笨 筌 答

答

220 道

ドウ
みち
road, way

道 combines *go* 辶 and *head, main* 首 to suggest going along a main path; i.e. a *road*.

Example sentences and meaning

1. way, path, street

* この道をまっすぐ行って下さい。
  Please go straight along this street.
* その店は国道246号線沿いにあります。
  That store is located on Highway 246.

2. moral principles, logic

* そんなこと道理に合わないよ。
  That's a load of nonsense!

3. way, religious teaching

* 道場は武道の稽古をするところです。
  A dojo is a place to practice martial arts.

Common compounds

鉄道	てつどう	railway
道徳	どうとく	ethics, morality
道路	どうろ	road, street, highway
歩道	ほどう	footpath, sidewalk
北海道	ほっかいどう	Hokkaidō

one stroke → 道 ← this stroke longer than those below it

12 ｜ ｀ ｿ ﾞ ﾞ ｢ ｢ ｢ 首 首 首 道 道

道

Quiz 28 (215-220)

A. Write in kanji

1. じかん ___ ___
2. ばしょ ___ 所
3. あきばれ ___ ___ ___
4. けさ ___ ___
5. くちごたえ ___ ___ ___
6. ほっかいどう ___ ___ ___
7. にんげん ___ ___
8. かいじょう 開 ___

B. Write in kanji

1. barometer ___ ___ ___
2. morning market ___ 市
3. reply, response ___ ___
4. calligraphy ___ ___
5. living room 居 ___
6. standpoint, position ___ ___
7. clear weather ___ ___
8. every morning ___ ___
9. piped water ___ ___
10. national highway ___ ___

C. Write in hiragana

1. 間に合う _____
2. 場面 _____
3. 晴れ晴れ _____
4. 平安朝 _____
5. 返答 _____
6. 歩道 _____
7. 昼間 _____
8. 競馬場 _____

221 買

バイ
か・う
buy

買 combines *net* ⺳ and *shells* 貝. Since shells were used for money, netting lots of shells meant being able to *buy* things.

Example sentences and meaning

1. buy

* A社がB社を買収した。
  Company A bought out Company B

* ちょっと買い物に行ってきます。
  I'm just going to do a bit of shopping.

2. evaluate

* 部長は彼の実績を買っている。
  The department chief is impressed with his performance.

3. invite, receive

* 彼は損な役を買って出た。
  He volunteered for the thankless job.

Common compounds

買い手	かいて	buyer
売買	ばいばい	buying and selling, trade
買値	かいね	purchase/bid price
買い占め	かいしめ	buy up, corner the market

買 ← top portion not 四
← end stroke firmly

12 ｜ 冂 冂 冃 罒 罒 严 罗 罗 罗 罗 買 買

買

---

222 番

バン
keeping watch, one's turn, number, order

番 combines *come* 来 and *field* 田, which can be thought of as coming to plant seedlings in a specific *order*.

Example sentences and meaning

1. order, number of times

* 次はあなたの番ですよ。
  It's your turn next.

* 待合室で順番を待った。
  I waited for my turn in the waiting room.

2. watch, guard

* 今日は留守番がいないんです。
  Today there's no one looking after the house.

* この犬は吠えないから番犬にならないよ。
  This dog is useless as a watchdog—it doesn't bark!

Common compounds

交番	こうばん	police box
番組	ばんぐみ	program
番号	ばんごう	number
番外	ばんがい	extra, outside
一番	いちばん	number one, most, first

番 来 portion slightly larger than 田 portion

12 ｜ ノ ⺍ 勹 坪 平 乎 来 来 釆 番 番 番

番

223 園 エン / その / garden

園 combines □ *enclosure* and 袁, originally a pictograph of a *kimono-clad woman*. The perfect place for such a woman is a *garden*.

Example sentences and meaning

1. plowed field, garden

* りんご園でりんご狩りをした。
I picked some apples at an orchard.

* 園芸用品は何階ですか。
What floor are the gardening supplies on?

2. place to enjoy oneself

* 金沢の兼六園という公園に行った。
I went to Kenrokuen Garden in Kanazawa.

3. place for learning

* 毎朝お母さんは子供を幼稚園に連れていきます。
Mothers take their children to the kindergarten every morning.

Common compounds

庭園	ていえん	garden
園長	えんちょう	head of a kindergarten
学園	がくえん	school, campus
動物園	どうぶつえん	zoo
園田	そのだ	Sonoda (name)

園 center vertical stroke does not end with a hook

13 丨 冂 冂 冂 冎 冎 甪 甫 甫 袁 園 園 園

園

224 遠 エン、*オン / とお・い / far, distant

遠 combines *go* ⻌ and *kimono-clad woman* 袁, perhaps referring to how *far* one must go to find a beautiful woman.

Example sentences and meaning

1. distant

* 思ったより駅から遠いなあ。
It's further from the station than I thought.

* ちょっと電話が遠いのですが。
(on the telephone) I can't hear you very well.

2. profound, unattainable

* 遠慮しないで召し上って下さい。
Please help yourself to the food.

* それはずいぶん遠大な計画だね。
That's quite an ambitious plan, isn't it?

Common compounds

遠足	えんそく	excursion, outing
敬遠	けいえん	shun, shy away
遠回り	とおまわり	detour, roundabout way
遠近感	えんきんかん	sense of perspective
望遠鏡	ぼうえんきょう	telescope

one stroke → 遠

13 一 十 士 吉 吉 吉 声 卓 卓 袁 袁 遠 遠

遠

225 楽

ガク、ラク
たの・しい、たの・しむ
fun, look forward to, music

楽 shows a *tree* 木 with lots of *white acorns* 楽, indicating an oak tree. Perhaps musical instruments were made from oak; *fun* evolved from making *music*.

Example sentences and meaning

1. music

* 何か楽器が演奏できますか。
Can you play any instruments?

* どんな音楽が好きですか。
What kind of music do you like?

2. pleasant, enjoyable

* 私は友達と会っておしゃべりを楽しんだ。
I met a friend and we had an enjoyable chat.

* 旅行は楽しかった？
Did you have good time on your trip?

* そこでは映画が最大の娯楽です。
Movies are the main form of entertainment there.

Common compounds

楽譜	がくふ	sheet music
気楽	きらく	feeling at ease, comfortable
苦楽	くらく	joys and sorrows
楽勝	らくしょう	easy victory
楽観的	らっかんてき	optimistic, hopeful

→ 楽 ← lower side strokes written starting from inside

13 ′ 亻 冇 白 白 白 泊 泊 泊 泊 楽 楽 楽

楽

226 新

シン
あたら・しい、あら・た、
*にい
new

新 can be thought of as using a *saw* 斤 to cut a *standing* 立 *tree* 木 in order to make a *new* building.

Example sentences and meaning

1. new

* 新年に新しい手帳を使う
to use a new daily planner for the new year

* 今朝の新聞読んだ？
Have you read this morning's newspaper?

* 新たな問題が起きた。
A new problem has come up.

2. renew, alter

* ビザを更新する
to renew one's visa

* 人事を一新する
to reorganize one's personnel

Common compounds

新鮮	しんせん	fresh
新築	しんちく	newly built
新人	しんじん	newcomer, new employee
新品	しんぴん	new article, brand new
*新妻	にいづま	newly married woman

新
end stroke firmly ↑↑ stroke tapers off

13 ′ 亠 亠 立 立 辛 辛 亲 新 新 新 新

新

Quiz 29 (221-226)

A. Match the kanji with its reading

1. 買値 ＿＿＿
2. 順番 ＿＿＿
3. 幼稚園 ＿＿＿
4. 望遠鏡 ＿＿＿
5. 楽観的 ＿＿＿
6. 新妻 ＿＿＿
7. 買収 ＿＿＿
8. 留守番 ＿＿＿

a. じゅんばん
b. るすばん
c. にいづま
d. かいね
e. ばいしゅう
f. らっかんてき
g. ようちえん
h. ぼうえんきょう

B. Write in English

1. 動物園 ＿＿＿＿＿＿＿＿＿＿＿＿
2. 遠回り ＿＿＿＿＿＿＿＿＿＿＿＿
3. 楽器 ＿＿＿＿＿＿＿＿＿＿＿＿
4. 更新 ＿＿＿＿＿＿＿＿＿＿＿＿
5. 売買 ＿＿＿＿＿＿＿＿＿＿＿＿
6. 番号 ＿＿＿＿＿＿＿＿＿＿＿＿
7. 庭園 ＿＿＿＿＿＿＿＿＿＿＿＿
8. 遠近感 ＿＿＿＿＿＿＿＿＿＿＿＿
9. 気楽 ＿＿＿＿＿＿＿＿＿＿＿＿
10. 新鮮 ＿＿＿＿＿＿＿＿＿＿＿＿

C. Write in kanji and kana

1. かいもの ＿＿ ＿＿ 物
2. こうばん ＿＿ ＿＿
3. がくえん ＿＿ ＿＿
4. えんそく ＿＿ ＿＿
5. おんがく ＿＿ ＿＿
6. しんぶん ＿＿ 聞
7. かいて ＿＿ ＿＿ ＿＿
8. いちばん ＿＿ ＿＿

227

数

スウ、*ス
かず、かぞ・える
number, count

数 combines *woman* 女, *rice* 米, and *stick in hand* 攵, and can be thought of as a woman *counting* rice with a stick.

Example sentences and meaning

1. number

* 棚卸しで商品の数を調べた。
  During inventory, we checked the number of items in stock.

* 多数決で議長を決めた。
  The chairperson was elected by majority decision.

2. count

* コピーの枚数を数える
  to count the number of copies

3. a few, several

* 本が届くのに数週間かかります。
  It takes several weeks for the books to arrive.

Common compounds

人数	にんずう	number of people
数学	すうがく	mathematics
数字	すうじ	digit, figures, numeral
少数	しょうすう	few, minority

数 ← stroke tapers off

13 ` ＇ ソ ゾ 米 米 米 娄 娄 娄 数 数 数

数

228 電 デン

electricity

電 shows *rain* 雨 with a flash of *lightning* 电 to represent *electricity*.

Example sentences and meaning

1. electricity

* 先月の電気代は高かった。
せんげつ でんきだい たか

Last month, the electricity bill was high.

2. telegraph, telephone

* 結婚式に行けないので祝電を打った。
けっこんしき い しゅくでん う

Because I couldn't attend the wedding reception, I sent a congratulatory telegram.

3. train

* 終電に間に合うかな。
しゅうでん ま あ

I wonder if I'll make the last train.

4. lightning

* 暗闇を裂いて電光が走った。
くらやみ さ でんこう

A flash of lightning cut through the darkness.

Common compounds

電池	でんち	battery, dry cell
電車	でんしゃ	train
電話	でんわ	telephone
電力	でんりょく	electric power
電子工学	でんしこうがく	electronics

電 ← stroke ends with hook

13　一　厂　厅　币　雨　雨　雨　雷　雷　雷　雷　雷　電

電

229 話 ワ

はなし、はな・す

speak, story

話 combines *words* 言 and *tongue* 舌 to give the meaning of *speak*.

Example sentences and meaning

1. speak, conversation

* あとで電話するよ。
でんわ

I'll phone you later.

* 英会話学校に一年間通った。
えいかいわがっこう いちねんかんかよ

I attended English conversation classes for a year.

2. story

* 「古事記」というのは日本の神話です。
こじき にほん しんわ

The *Kojiki* is a Japanese collection of myths.

3. circumstances, situations

* 彼は話のわかる人だよ。
かれ はなし ひと

He's one who understands the situation.

Common compounds

話題	わだい	topic, subject
世話	せわ	assistance, take care of
実話	じつわ	true story
童話	どうわ	children's story, fairy tale
昔話	むかしばなし	legend, folk tale

話 ← stroke tapers down from right to left

13　丶　亠　亠　言　言　言　言　訂　訂　話　話　話

話

230 歌
カ
うた、うた・う
song, sing

歌 combines *open mouth* 欠 and two 可, pronounced "ka". "Ka-ka" was the Chinese version of "tra-la-la," which suggests *singing*.

Example sentences and meaning

1. song, sing

* 鼻歌を歌いながら運転している
  to hum songs while driving
* 私の好きな歌手が来日した。
  A singer that I like came to Japan.
* 国歌が演奏されるときには起立する
  to stand when the national anthem is performed

2. *waka* (Japanese poem)

* 母は和歌に興味があります。
  My mother is interested in *waka* poems.

Common compounds

歌詞	かし	lyrics
演歌	えんか	*enka* (Japanese ballad)
賛美歌	さんびか	hymn
歌舞伎	かぶき	Kabuki
歌劇	かげき	opera

歌
stroke ends with hook→

14	ー	'	亻	亓	曱	亘	曱	酉	哥	哥	歌	歌	歌

歌

231 語
ゴ
かた・る、かた・らう
word, talk

語 can be thought of as a *mouth* 口 saying *five* 五 *words* 言, a reference to *talking*.

Example sentences and meaning

1. speak

* 彼は語気を荒げて反論した。
  He argued back angrily.
* 寝る前に父はおもしろい話を語ってくれた。
  My father used to tell me interesting stories before going to sleep.

2. language, words

* 中国語を習う
  to learn Chinese
* あの人は語学力を買われている。
  He is highly valued for his linguistic skill.
* 日本語で外来語がたくさん使われています。
  There are many foreign loanwords in Japanese.

Common compounds

物語	ものがたり	story, tale
語彙	ごい	vocabulary
敬語	けいご	honorific language
言語学	げんごがく	linguistics
国語辞典	こくごじてん	Japanese dictionary

語
not 話

14	`	亠	亠	亖	吉	言	言	訂	訢	証	証	語	語

語

232 算

サン

calculate

算 originated from a pictograph of *two hands* 廾 holding a *bamboo* 竹 *abacus* 目, a reference to *calculating*.

Example sentences and meaning

1. count

* 来年度の予算をたてる
  to make the budget for the coming year

* 私は暗算が苦手です。
  I'm not good at calculating in my head.

2. measure, scheme, plan, estimate

* 失業が増える公算が大きい。
  There is a strong chance that unemployment will increase.

Common compounds

算数	さんすう	arithmetic, math
算出	さんしゅつ	calculation, computation
決算	けっさん	settlement (of accounts)
通算	つうさん	summing up, the sum total
目算	もくさん	expectation, estimate

stroke tapers off → 算

| 14 | ノ | ト | ナ | ケ | ヤ | 竹 | 竹 | 竹 | 竹 | 笪 | 笪 | 算 | 算 |

算						

Test 9 (161-232)

A. Write in kanji and kana

1. mathematics ___ ___
2. electric power ___ ___
3. assistance, take care of 世 ___
4. singer ___ ___
5. Chinese language ___ ___ ___
6. arithmetic, math ___ ___
7. several weeks ___ ___ ___
8. a flash of lightning ___ ___
9. national anthem ___ ___
10. linguistic skill ___ ___ ___
11. chance, probability ___ ___
12. waterfowl, aquatic bird ___ ___
13. rain cloud ___ ___
14. field, branch ___ ___
15. midway ___ ___
16. case, circumstances ___ ___
17. periods of clear weather ___ ___ ___
18. this morning ___ ___
19. martial arts school ___ ___
20. watchdog ___ ___

B. Write in hiragana

1. 多数決 _____
2. 電子工学 _____
3. 英会話 _____
4. 賛美歌 _____
5. 物語 _____
6. 予算 _____
7. 園長 _____
8. 娯楽 _____
9. 新品 _____
10. 組閣 _____
11. 鳥肌 _____
12. 野菜 _____
13. 総理大臣 _____
14. 雲集 _____
15. 油絵 _____
16. 滞在期間 _____
17. 牧場 _____
18. 晴れ着 _____
19. 朝ご飯 _____
20. 解答 _____

C. Write in kanji

1. すうじ ___ ___
2. でんしゃ ___ ___

3. わか ___
4. がいらいご ___ ___ ___
5. さんしゅつ ___ ___
6. にんずう ___ ___
7. でんち ___ ___
8. げんごがく ___ ___ ___
9. くうかん ___ ___
10. たちば ___ ___
11. どうり ___ ___
12. ばいばい ___ ___
13. ばんぐみ ___ ___
14. そのだ ___ ___
15. きらく ___ ___
16. しんじん ___ ___
17. やまぐちぐみ ___ ___ ___
18. はくちょう ___ ___
19. ひるま ___ ___
20. でんわ ___ ___

D. Match the kanji with its reading

1. 枚数 ___   a. あんざん
2. 電気代 ___   b. しんわ
3. 昔話 ___   c. そうちょう
4. 鼻歌 ___   d. まいすう
5. 国語辞典 ___   e. けっさん
6. 暗算 ___   f. けいご
7. 少数 ___   g. にほんご
8. 神話 ___   h. がくふ
9. 歌舞伎 ___   i. どうろ
10. 敬語 ___   j. でんきだい
11. 決算 ___   k. しょうすう
12. 競馬場 ___   l. ばんがい
13. 早朝 ___   m. はなうた
14. 道路 ___   n. えんりょ
15. 番外 ___   o. こくごじてん
16. 園芸用品 ___   p. けいばじょう
17. 遠慮 ___   q. しんちく
18. 楽譜 ___   r. かぶき
19. 新築 ___   s. えんげいようひん
20. 日本語 ___   t. むかしばなし

E. Rewrite using as many kanji as possible

1. あす はれ だったら、ばばくん と いっしょ に にっこう へ え を かき に いく。

_____

2. せんしゅう、しょうがくせいたち が あ
   の こうえん の なか で たのしく
   うた を うたっていた。

_____

3. 今、しゅう に にかい あたらしい イ
   タリアご の かいわ の ばんぐみ を
   テレビ で やっている。

_____

4. けさ、あめ が ふった あと だった
   ので、ものすごい かず の ことり が
   つち の なか から でてきた むし
   を たべていた。

_____

5. とおい ゆきぐに へ いった とき で
   んしゃ で なんじかん も かかった。

_____

6. のぐちさん は きゅうじつ に ゴルフ
   を して たのしんでいる。

_____

7. あさ おきる と くも ひとつ なく
   て、とても いい きぶん に なった。
   それで、ぼく の いえ の まえ の
   みちを ずっと やま まで あるく こ
   と に した。

_____

8. たかやませんせい が はなしている あ
   いだ に こうこうせい の やく はん
   ぶん が ねてしまった。

_____

9. とりやまくん は その できごと を
   みてきた か の よう に かたった。

_____

10. げんき に うたいながら しょうねんた
    ち は まるた を くんで こや を
    つくった。

_____

233 読

ドク、トク、*トウ
よ・む
read

読 combines *sell* 売 and *words* 言, perhaps referring to books, which are *read*.

Example sentences and meaning

1. read

* 毎朝新聞を三紙読む
  to read three newspapers every morning
* 音読みと訓読み
  the Chinese and Japanese readings of characters

2. infer, guess the meaning

* 行間を読む
  to read between the lines
* 彼は読みが深い。
  He possesses keen insight.

Common compounds

読書	どくしょ	reading
解読	かいどく	deciphering, decoding
読解力	どっかいりょく	reading comprehension
読唇術	どくしんじゅつ	lip reading
*句読点	くとうてん	punctuation mark

left bottom stroke of 売 tapers off → 読 ← stroke ends with hook

14 ｀ ㆍ ㆍ 亠 亠 言 言 言 訓 計 詰 詰 詰 読

読

234 聞

ブン、モン
き・く、き・こえる
hear

聞 combines *gate* 門 and *ear* 耳, and suggests *listening* at a gate.

Example sentences and meaning

1. hear, listen to, ask

* 山でカッコーの声が聞こえた。
  I heard cuckoos calling in the mountains.
* 見聞を広めるために旅行する
  to travel so as to add to one's experience

2. rumor, reputation

* あまり人聞きの悪いことは言わないでよ。
  You shouldn't talk about such gossipy things!

Common compounds

聞き手	ききて	listener
新聞	しんぶん	newspaper
風聞	ふうぶん	report, rumor
外聞	がいぶん	reputation, respectability
聴聞会	ちょうもんかい	public hearing

聞 ← bottom stroke for 耳 does not protrude

14 ｜ ｜ ｢ ｢ ｢ 門 門 門 門 閂 閂 閏 聞 聞

聞

235

鳴

メイ
な・く、な・る、な・らす

cry, sing (by animals), ring

鳴 combines *mouth* 口 and *bird* 鳥 to represent a *bird singing*.

Example sentences and meaning

1. singing or crying of birds, animals, insects

* 猫の鳴き声がうるさくて眠れなかった。
  I couldn't sleep because of the cat's yowling.

2. sound, ring

* 今朝は目覚まし時計が鳴らなかった。
  My alarm clock didn't go off this morning.

* クラリネットを鳴らす
  to play the clarinet

3. enjoy wide popularity

* 大学時代は卓球で鳴らしたものです。
  In my university days, I was well-known for playing ping-pong.

Common compounds

共鳴	きょうめい	resonance, sympathy
鳴動	めいどう	rumbling
雷鳴	らいめい	thunder
鳴門	なると	whirlpool

note position of dots → 鳴

14	丨	口	口	口ˊ	叮	叮	咟	嗎	嗎	嗎	鳴	鳴

鳴

236

線

セン

line

線 combines *thread* 糸 and *water spring* 泉 to suggest a *thin stream of water*. From this came the meaning of *line*.

Example sentences and meaning

1. line

* 台風で電線が切れた。
  The power lines were severed by the typhoon.

* 点線のところで紙を折って下さい。
  Fold the paper along the dotted line.

2. traffic route

* 線路に靴が落ちた。
  A shoe fell on the railway track.

3. line representing an end, limit

* 水平線がよく見える。
  There's a good view of the horizon.

4. policy

* その線で交渉してみよう。
  Let's try and negotiate along these lines.

Common compounds

直線	ちょくせん	straight line
曲線	きょくせん	curve
無線	むせん	wireless, radio
視線	しせん	one's gaze, line of vision
新幹線	しんかんせん	the bullet train

線 center stroke ends with hook

15	ˊ	乡	幺	乡	糸	糸	糸	紒	組	紵	綧	綧	線

線

237 親

シン
おや、した・しい、
した・しむ

close, intimate, parent

親 combines *stand* 立, *tree* 木, and *look* 見, which can be thought of as standing to look *closely* at a tree.

Example sentences and meaning

1. **parent(s)**
* ご両親はお元気ですか。
Are your parents well?
* 親会社と子会社
parent company and subsidiary company
* 親指にけがをして何もできない。
I've hurt my thumb and can't do anything.

2. **relative, blood relation**
* お正月には親類が大勢集まった。
We had a large family get-together on New Year's.

3. **intimate**
* 親しい友だちが外国に行ってしまった。
A close friend of mine went overseas.

Common compounds

母親	ははおや	mother
肉親	にくしん	blood relationship
親分	おやぶん	boss (gangster)
親切	しんせつ	kind, friendly
親友	しんゆう	close friend

親 ← stroke ends with hook

16 ｀ 一 ｀ 立 立 辛 辛 辛 亲 亲 釗 釠 朝 親 親

---

238 頭

トウ、ズ、＊ト
あたま

head

頭 combines 頁 *head* and 豆 *stand*. The stand suggests a *vessel*, which due to its shape reinforced the meaning of *head*.

Example sentences and meaning

1. **head**
* 頭が痛い。
I have a headache.

2. **the first, the start**
* 彼は列の先頭に立っていた。
He was standing at the front of the line.

3. **head of a group**
* 頭取というのは銀行の社長のことです。
Tōdori refers to the president of a bank.

4. **counter for large animals**
* 牧場には馬が八頭いる。
There are eight horses in the meadow.

Common compounds

頭金	あたまきん	down payment, deposit
頭脳	ずのう	brains, head
頭痛	ずつう	headache
店頭	てんとう	shop front, shop window

stroke goes up from left to right → 頭

16 一 一 一 一 豆 豆 豇 豇 豇 頭 頭 頭 頭

239 顔

ガン
かお
face

顔 combines *head* 頁 and *handsome* 彦, which came from a pictograph of a forehead and three hairs. Handsome head took on the meaning of *face*.

Example sentences and meaning

1. face

* 顔(かお)を洗(あら)ってクリームをつける
  to wash one's face and apply cream
* 顔色(かおいろ)が悪(わる)いけど、大丈夫(だいじょうぶ)?
  You look pale. Are you all right?

2. expression, appearance

* 彼女(かのじょ)は知(し)らん顔(かお)で通(とお)りすぎて行(い)った。
  She ignored me and walked right past.
* 顔(かお)をつぶされる
  to lose face

Common compounds

顔負け	かおまけ	put to shame, be outdone
顔つき	かおつき	looks, expression
顔料	がんりょう	pigment, cosmetics
洗顔	せんがん	washing one's face
笑顔	えがお	smiling face

顔 three strokes for 彡 taper down from right to left

18 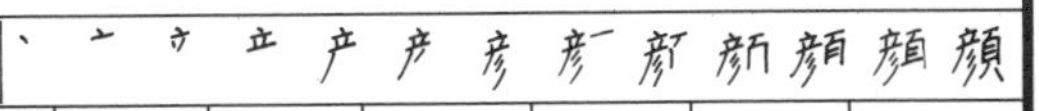

顔

240 曜

ヨウ
day of the week

曜 combines *sun* 日, *bird* 隹, and *two wings* ヨヨ, suggesting the sun flying like a bird; i.e., the passing of a *day*.

Example sentences and meaning

1. day of the week

* やっと金曜日(きんようび)だね。
  Friday is here at last.
* 今日(きょう)は何曜日(なんようび)だっけ?
  What day is it today?
* 第二第四土曜日(だいにだいよんどようび)はお休(やす)みです。
  The second and fourth Saturdays are holidays.
* 火曜定休(かようていきゅう)
  Closed Tuesdays

Common compounds

曜日	ようび	day of the week
日曜日	にちようび	Sunday
月曜日	げつようび	Monday
水曜日	すいようび	Wednesday

日 is narrow → 曜

18 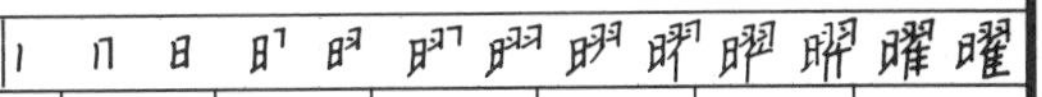

曜

Quiz 30 (233-240)

A. Write in hiragana
1. 読解力　_____
2. 風聞　_____
3. 雷鳴　_____
4. 水平線　_____
5. 親会社　_____
6. 先頭　_____
7. 知らん顔　_____
8. 何曜日　_____

B. Write in kanji and kana
1. どくしょ　　___ ___
2. ききて　　___ ___ ___
3. なきごえ　　___ ___ ___
4. でんせん　　___ ___
5. しんゆう　　___友
6. あたまきん　　___ ___
7. かおいろ　　___ ___ ___
8. すいようび　　___ ___ ___
9. くんよみ　　訓___ ___
10. がいぶん　　___ ___

C. Match the kanji with its English meaning
1. whirlpool ___   a. 新聞
2. dotted line ___   b. 金曜日
3. kind, friendly ___   c. 親切
4. bank president ___   d. 洗顔
5. washing ___   e. 鳴門
   one's face
6. Friday ___   f. 解読
7. deciphering, ___   g. 点線
   decoding
8. newspaper ___   h. 頭取り

Review Test 3

Review Test 3 (161-240)

A. Write in kanji and kana

1. よみかた ___ ___ ___
2. ははおや ___ ___
3. しんぶん ___ ___
4. しらんかお ___ ___ ___
5. にちようび ___ ___ ___
6. てんちょう ___ ___
7. ちょくせん ___ ___
8. あかり ___ ___
9. きょうかしょ ___ ___ ___
10. にほんかい ___ ___ ___
11. せいかつ ___ ___
12. ごうけい ___ ___
13. こうはん ___ ___
14. おもいだす ___ ___ ___ ___
15. しつがい ___ ___
16. てくび ___ ___
17. あきばれ ___ ___ ___
18. きにゅう ___ ___
19. みなみかぜ ___ ___ ___
20. とけい ___ ___

B. Write in hiragana

1. 句読点 _____
2. 見聞 _____
3. 鳴動 _____
4. 新幹線 _____
5. 親指 _____
6. 頭痛 _____
7. 笑顔 _____
8. 月曜日 _____
9. 点検 _____
10. 南向き _____
11. 風景画 _____
12. 帰化 _____
13. 原稿 _____
14. 高価 _____
15. 折り紙 _____
16. 自殺 _____
17. 書斎 _____
18. 手紙一通 _____
19. 鮮魚 _____
20. 勉強 _____

C. Write in kanji and kana

1. reading ___ ___
2. a cry, call ___ ___ ___
3. power lines ___ ___

4. boss (gangster) ___ ___
5. shop front, shop window ___ ___
6. looks, expression ___ ___
7. What day? ___ ___
8. Christianity ___ ___ ___

9. assembly, construction ___ ___

10. bird cage
11. Ueno ___ ___
12. rain cloud ___ ___
13. one week ___ ___
14. footpath, sidewalk ___ ___
15. buyer ___ ___
16. police box ___ ___
17. apple orchard ___ ___

18. ambitious plan ___ ___ ___

19. music ___ ___
20. newcomer,
    new employee ___ ___

D. Write in English

1. 訓読み _____
2. 聴聞会 _____
3. 共鳴 _____
4. 無線 _____
5. 肉親 _____
6. 頭脳 _____
7. 顔負け _____
8. 木曜日 _____
9. 成長 _____
10. 直接 _____
11. 店員 _____
12. 歩行 _____
13. 梅雨明け _____
14. 専門 _____
15. 作夜 _____
16. 百科事典 _____
17. 海岸 _____
18. 活動 _____
19. 小計 _____
20. 後世 _____

E. Match the kanji with its reading

1. 線路 ___ a. あんしつ

2.	両親	___	b.	せいじか
3.	顔料	___	c.	なつじかん
4.	水曜日	___	d.	こうねつ
5.	思い出	___	e.	せんろ
6.	暗室	___	f.	もうしこみしょ
7.	部首	___	g.	きけつ
8.	秋刀魚	___	h.	りょうしん
9.	政治家	___	i.	がくふう
10.	記録	___	j.	じそく
11.	欠点	___	k.	がんりょう
12.	学風	___	l.	じゃくてん
13.	夏時間	___	m.	しへい
14.	帰結	___	n.	すいようび
15.	原因	___	o.	ぶしゅ
16.	高熱	___	p.	げんいん
17.	紙幣	___	q.	けってん
18.	時速	___	r.	おもいで
19.	弱点	___	s.	さんま
20.	申込書	___	t.	きろく

F. Match the kanji with its English meaning

1.	音楽通	___	a.	last week
2.	淡水魚	___	b.	meal, dining
3.	教授	___	c.	Maebashi
4.	親類	___	d.	wild, savage
5.	黒子	___	e.	summing up, the sum total
6.	先週	___	f.	thorough knowledge of music
7.	除雪	___	g.	preamble
8.	漁船	___	h.	(black) tea
9.	早春	___	i.	topic, subject
10.	食事	___	j.	fishing boat
11.	星占い	___	k.	relative, relation
12.	前橋	___	l.	early spring
13.	紅茶	___	m.	lunch
14.	昼食	___	n.	freshwater fish
15.	通算	___	o.	lyrics
16.	歌詞	___	p.	astrology, horoscope
17.	話題	___	q.	snow removal
18.	定食	___	r.	professor
19.	野生	___	s.	mole (facial)
20.	前文	___	t.	set course meal

G. Rewrite using as many kanji as possible

1. とおく から うたごえ が かすか に
きこえてきた。

_____

2. この ごろ いたずら でんわ が おお
くて、あたま に きている よ。

_____

3. すいようび に おや から てがみ が
きて、すぐ に よんで、へんじ を だ
した。

_____

4. ブザー を なんかい ならして も、こ
たえ が なかった。

_____

5. いもうと が その おもしろい はなし
を きいた とき、かお を まっか に
して、おおごえ で わらった。

_____

6. さいきん、あさ、ひる、ばん、さんかい
しろい ごはん を たべている にほん
じん が すくなく なってきている。

_____

7. すいへいせん の すこし うえ に つ
る が さんわ とんでいた。そして ま
もなく まるで くろい てん の よ
う に なって みえなくなった。

_____

8. こんど は なかむらさん の よむ ば
ん だ から よく きいて ください
ね。

_____

9. ドイツご の きょうかしょ の え の
のった ページ を かぞえてみたら
じゅうよん ページ ほど あった。

_____

10. らいしゅう の げつようび は おかあ
さん の たんじょうび だ から きれ
い な でんき スタンド を かってあ
げよう か な。

_____

11. こうえん どおり を まっすぐ あるい
たら こうばん に つく。しょどうよう
の よい かみ を うっている みせ
は その すぐ ちかく に ある。

_____

12. この みなみ の しま は てんごく
みたい！まっさお な うみ で、そら
に は くも ひとつ なく、よる ほし
が きらきら かがやいていて、くに
へかえる き が しない。

_____

13. おてら の もん の まえ に あらた
に おちゃ の おいしい みせ が で
きた。

_____

14. こうじょう の サイレン が しょうご
に なる と、ひるやすみ に なる。

_____

15. じゅうがつ みっか の しめきり に
ま に あう よう に、すぐ この ば
で かいて だして ください。

_____

16. くろかわさん は しんがた の じどう
しゃ の いっかげつ の うりあげ が
やく ろくせんまんえん と けいさん
した。

_____

17. おととい したしい ゆうじん の その
だくん が なつよう の きいろい
シャツ を かってくれた。

_____

18. たかぎさん の いえ は その ほそい
とおり を いって、ふたつめ の かど
を みぎ に まがる と、すぐ わかる
と おもいます よ。

_____

19. あっ と いう ま に かぜ が つよ
く なって、とり の なきごえ が き
こえなくなった。

_____

20. しゅうまつ に ふね で とおい しま
へ いって、さかな つり を して、き
を はらした。

_____

Answers

Answers

Quiz 1

A.
1. にほんいち　　2. ひとり　　3. にがつ　　4. にきゅう　　5. しちねんかん、ななねんかん　　6. ようか
7. きゅうしゅう　　8. くじ

B.
1. 一回　　2. 一年　　3. 二人　　4. 二十歳　　5. 七五三　　6. 八百屋　　7. 九日間　　8. 十月　　9. 二度
10. 十分

C.
1. one page/copy　　2. two weeks　　3. second generation, second name　　4. 22　　5. many different voices
6. everybody's friend　　7. 20th day of the month, 20 days　　8. Tanabata Festival

Quiz 2

A.
1. なこうど　　2. にゅうがく　　3. じつりょく　　4. みかづき　　5. せんえんさつ　　6. せんにん
7. けんりょく　　8. いりぐち

B.
1. 入院　　2. 努力　　3. 三重県　　4. 三千円　　5. 上がる　　6. 上野　　7. 上等　　8. 何人　　9. 三角
10. 日本人

C.
1. ドイツ人　　2. 輸入　　3. 売り上げ　　4. 千代田区　　5. 三ヶ月　　6. 協力　　7. 力士　　8. 上手

Quiz 3

A.
1. Please　　2. the end of July　　3. adult　　4. Odawara (place)　　5. population　　6. child　　7. university
8. unskillful, poor at

B.
1. 大問題　　2. 陛下　　3. 小学校　　4. 早口　　5. 火山　　6. 迷子　　7. 口座　　8. 改札口　　9. 値下がり
10. 富士山

C.
1. かせん　　2. たいせつ　　3. こぎって　　4. ひじょうぐち　　5. やまなしけん　　6. ようす　　7. くちべに
8. りし

Test 1

A.
1. 王女　　2. 夕食　　3. 川崎　　4. 五ヶ月　　5. 六時　　6. 一週間　　7. 七夕　　8. 十月三十一日　　9. 人気
10. 十分

B.
1. ゆうがた　　2. さつきばれ　　3. だいろっかん　　4. めがみ　　5. かわさき　　6. にゅうこく　　7. さんかく
8. いっせんまんえん　　9. じょうず　　10. ねあげ

C.
1. 小包　　2. 入り口　　3. 登山　　4. 王子　　5. 土日　　6. 五千十円　　7. 六日　　8. 女の子　　9. 子会社
10. 実力

D.
1. put money in your bank account　　2. take a bath　　3. go up stairs　　4. go down a mountain　　5. The University of
Tōkyō　　6. a singer who can do many different voices　　7. the girl came twice　　8. go to Japan on November 7

E.
1. 山での夕焼けはきれいですね。
　　The afterglow of the sun in the mountains is pretty.
2. 川上さんと田口さんではどちらが年上でしょうか。
　　Who is older, Mr. Kawakami or Mr. Taguchi?

3. 小田原で小型のトラックを七台見ました。
   I saw seven small-sized trucks in Odawara.
4. 六本木の土地の値段は最近下がりましたか。
   Recently have the land prices in Roppongi gone down?
5. 「お土産に何がいいんですか。」「小さい人形を下さい。」
   Is there anything I can get you while I'm on my trip? A small doll, please
6. 五月五日は子供の日です。
   May 5 is Children's Day.
7. 今二十八歳です。
   I'm 28 years old.
8. 川口さんにオレンジを三つ上げました。
   I gave Mr. Kawaguchi three oranges.
9. 「あそこに女性が何人いますか。」「二人います。」
   How many women are over there? There are two.
10. その大きい本の下に山口さんの手紙がありますか。
    Is Mr. Yamaguchi's letter under that big book?

Quiz 4

A.

1. draw a circle　　2. prince　　3. fire　　4. monthly income　　5. seeing eye dog　　6. method　　7. king
8. last month

B

1. てつだう　　2. あきたけん　　3. しょうがつ　　4. ぼうか　　5. エリザベスじょおう　　6. えんまん
7. こいぬ　　8. てりょうり　　9. てんか　　10. きゅうじゅうえんのきっぷ

C.

1. 円高　　2. 王様　　3. 花火　　4. 三ケ月　　5. 犬小屋　　6. 手に入れる　　7. 今月　　8. 火をつける

Quiz 5

A.

1. すいどうだい　　2. でんわちゅう　　3. にちじょうかいわ　　4. てんじょう　　5. もじ　　6. さくらのき
7. てんきよほう　　8. なかゆび

B.

1. 水　　2. 世界中　　3. 昨日　　4. 天国　　5. 文学　　6. 木の葉　　7. 明日　　8. 天文台　　9. 水曜日
10. 木材

C.

1. g　　2. h　　3. f　　4. a　　5. d　　6. b　　7. e　　8. c

Quiz 6

A.

1. 四方八方　　2. 右目　　3. 左足　　4. 五十円玉　　5. 出口　　6. お正月　　7. 手紙を出す　　8. 四人

B.

1. さゆう　　2. みずたまもよう　　3. しゅっちょう　　4. しょうご　　5. いえをでる　　6. せいじょう
7. ひだりきき　　8. よんじゅっかい　　9. みぎうで　　10. せいかく

C

1. 四国　　2. 右折　　3. 左手　　4. 玉座　　5. 外出　　6. 訂正　　7. 出席　　8. 左側

Test 2

A.

1. 中学生　　2. 大きな石　　3. 水田　　4. 白人　　5. 本日　　6. 目的　　7. 八十七円　　8. 火山　　9. 先月
10. 番犬　　11. 上手　　12. 生ビール　　13. 宝石　　14. 本田　　15. 白い車

Answers

B.
1. ほんしゅう　　2. めじるし　　3. いけばな　　4. いっせきにちょう　　5. でんえん　　6. しろくろ　　7. きほん
8. にばんめ　　9. すいどう　　10. とちゅう　　11. みっかめ　　12. てんさい　　13. ぶんか　　14. もくぞう
15. もんく

C.
1. flower arrangement　　2. petroleum　　3. country, rural areas　　4. confess　　5. true, real　　6. focus of attention
7. teacher, doctor　　8. hardheaded　　9. offshore oil field　　10. blank sheet　　11. real　　12. Chinese cabbage
13. square　　14. right-handed　　15. left side

D.
1. f　　2. j　　3. n　　4. b　　5. i　　6. o　　7. m　　8. a　　9. e　　10. h　　11. l　　12. c　　13. g
14. k　　15. d

E.
1. 日本で生まれた。　　2. 石川さんの大きな口　　3. 川口さん田舎のいえ　　4. 白黒のテレビをうって下さい。
5. 本しゃは山口けんにある。　　6. 一人目の子ども　　7. 九百円の本をかった。　　8. 三がいで火じがおきた。
9. こん月はなん月ですか。　　10. 手まがかかりますね。　　11. このとけいは水ぎんでんちをつかう。
12. 生ビールの中ジョッキ　　13. 今日は石田くんのたん生日だ。　　14. このまちは天ごくだ。
15. 日本ごのテキスト

F.
1. 川田さんの白い犬に左手をかまれた。
   My left hand was bitten by Mr. Kawada's white dog.
2. 子どもが五人水の中から石をひろって出てきた。
   Five children came out of the water with stones they had picked up.
3. 四つかどを右にまがると大きな天文台があります。
   If you turn right at the crossroads, you'll find a large observtory.
4. 田中さんのところに子犬が生まれたそうです。
   I heard that puppies were born at Mr. Tanaka's place.
5. 五十円玉が八まいで百円のものが四つかえます。
   With eight ¥50 coins, I can buy four things that cost ¥100.
6. 山火事のあとで木がなかなか生えてこなかった。
   After the fire on the mountain, the trees didn't grow back for a long time.
7. 小さな王女さまの目は大きくてかわいい。
   That little princess is cute with her big eyes.
8. 月の中に生きものがすんでいると日本ではいわれています。
   In Japan it is said that there are things living in the moon.
9. 夕方になると山のむこうにほしがみえてきます。
   When it becomes evening, you can see the stars fan out behind the mountain.
10. 六番の出口をとおって七番の入り口から入って下さい。
    Go past exit six and go in through exit seven.

Quiz 7
A.
1. 国立大学　　2. 五百円玉　　3. 去年　　4. 電気　　5. 名古屋　　6. 先日　　7. 八百屋　　8. 定年

B.
1. 病気　　2. 名前　　3. 先生　　4. 対立　　5. 三百人　　6. 少年　　7. 気圧　　8. 名刺　　9. お先に　　10. 先月

C.
1. independence　　2. encyclopedia　　3. the 50's　　4. short temper　　5. well-known　　6. one's senior, superior
7. surname　　8. annual income

Quiz 8
A.
1. はやおき　　2. ひとやすみ　　3. かんじ　　4. けいと　　5. たけのこ　　6. むしめがね　　7. あかじ
8. きゅうけい

B.
1. fast talking　　2. consecutive holidays　　3. subtitles　　4. silk thread　　5. bamboo sword　　6. reptiles

7. quick, light-footed   8. day off   9. figure, numeral   10. beginning, clue

C.
1. g   2. d   3. a   4. b   5. h   6. e   7. f   8. c

Quiz 9
A.
1. 耳鳴り   2. 発見   3. 港町   4. 電車   5. 中村   6. 男の子   7. 見本   8. 田舎町

B.
1. じびか   2. いけん   3. ちょうちょうせんきょ   4. ちゅうしゃきんし   5. ぎょそん   6. だんせいよう
7. みみがとおい   8. きしゃかいけん   9. じどうしゃ   10. むいそん

C.
1. first I've heard of it   2. show   3. row of stores and houses   4. start, departure (of a train)   5. villager
6. eldest son   7. man, male, boy   8. garage

Test 3
A.
1. 不足   2. 赤道   3. 花火   4. 巻き貝   5. 入学   6. 現金   7. 遠足   8. 赤ちゃん   9. 生け花
10. 大学   11. 金曜日   12. 中立   13. 百足   14. 八十五年   15. 空気   16. 氏名   17. 先生   18. 早番
19. 夏休み   20. 泣き虫

B.
1. まんぞく   2. まっか   3. はなよめ   4. あかがい   5. りゅうがく   6. りょうきん   7. あしがながい
8. せきがいせん   9. かいか   10. かいのさしみ   11. しんりがく   12. ぜいきん   13. けいと
14. たけぐし   15. ぼうちゅうざい   16. パンのみみ   17. けんぶつ   18. よんちょうめ   19. すいしゃ
20. そんちょう

C.
1. 次男   2. 足りない   3. 赤らめる   4. 花びら   5. 二枚貝   6. 学校   7. 税金   8. 立春   9. 八百屋
10. 近年   11. 天気   12. 名字   13. 先月   14. 早川   15. 休日   16. 赤十字   17. 糸を引く
18. 竹の子   19. 本の虫   20. 初耳

D.
1. c   2. o   3. k   4. m   5. f   6. i   7. n   8. a   9. l   10. q   11. b   12. r   13. t   14. e
15. p   16. g   17. s   18. h   19. j   20. d

E.
1. ストッキング二足
   two pairs of stockings
2. 赤い花を下さい。
   A red flower, please.
3. まき貝と赤貝をひろった。
   I gathered some conches and ark shells
4. 大学でスペインごを学ぶ
   to study Spanish at a university
5. お金を金こに入れる
   put money in a safe
6. 三足す七は十です。
   Three plus seven equals ten.
7. か学とすう学のクラスを休む
   not go to one's chemistry and math classes
8. その金ぱつの女せいは赤のた人です。
   That blond woman is a complete stranger to me.
9. あの本やで学生が二人立ちよみをしている。
   There are two students standing in that book store reading.
10. 立ぱな金ぞくでできたバッジ百こをかいました。
    I bought one hundred fine badges made of metal.

Answers

Quiz 10

A.
1. ほしぞら　　2. せいしゅんじだい　　3. こばやし　　4. こさめ　　5. たばこ　　6. はつおん　　7. こうこう
8. しんりんかいはつ

B.
1. 空手　　2. 青森　　3. 松林　　4. 長雨　　5. 海草　　6. 足音　　7. 小学校　　8. 森田　　9. 音楽　　10. 梅雨

C.
1. 空白　　2. 青空　　3. 林道　　4. 大雨　　5. 草むしり　　6. 音声　　7. 校正　　8. 録音

Review Test 1

A.
1. なりたくうこう　　2. まっさお　　3. りんぎょう　　4. つ¢‰　　5. みちくさ　　6. おんよみ　　7. しょこう
8. しんりんしげん　　9. みみたぶ　　10. みかた　　11. まちやくば　　12. しゃこ　　13. のうそん　　14. おおお
とこ　　15. そうちょう　　16. ねんじゅうむきゅう　　17. じてん　　18. いとへん　　19. あおだけ
20. なんきんむし

B.
1. empty taxi　　2. youth　　3. dense forest, jungle　　4. heavy rain, downpour　　5. pioneer　　6. record
7. prep school　　8. woods, forest　　9. coexist, be compatible　　10. pack of lies　　11. New Year's card
12. energy, vitality　　13. noted product, speciality　　14. priority, preference　　15. the four seasons　　16. right hand
17. left turn　　18. balancing on a ball　　19. home delivery (from a restaurant)　　20. justice

C.
1. 空気　　2. 青木　　3. 小林　　4. 小雨　　5. 雑草　　6. 音楽　　7. 学校　　8. 中森　　9. 水曜日　　10. 中学生
11. 元日　　12. 天野　　13. 作文　　14. 松林　　15. 三千円　　16. 女王　　17. 火山　　18. 今月　　19. 子犬
20. 両手

D.
1. 羽田空港　　2. 青森　　3. 風雨　　4. 草食　　5. 発音　　6. 予備校　　7. 森林開発　　8. 下着　　9. 最大
10. 小学校　　11. 非常口　　12. 富士山　　13. 王子　　14. 人気　　15. 入社　　16. 力作　　17. 三月三日
18. 千円札　　19. 向上　　20. 一週間

E.
1. c　　2. f　　3. l　　4. q　　5. a　　6. n　　7. b　　8. m　　9. t　　10. s　　11. h　　12. o　　13. g
14. k　　15. r　　16. d　　17. j　　18. p　　19. i　　20. e

F.
1. e　　2. j　　3. s　　4. p　　5. i　　6. d　　7. t　　8. o　　9. h　　10. f　　11. n　　12. q　　13. a
14. l　　15. g　　16. c　　17. r　　18. m　　19. k　　20. b

G.
1. 足の長い男の子
   a long-legged boy
2. 村上さんの赤い車を見せて下さい。
   Please show me Mr. Murakami's red car.
3. 日本人は本とうに生たまごをたべるのがすきですか。
   Do Japanese people really like to eat raw eggs?
4. さく日田中くんは森林学の本を手に入れた。
   Tanaka got hold of a book on forestry yesterday.
5. 1983年、十月二十四日火よう日に川口先生はゆう名な百か字てんを出ぱんした。
   On Tuesday, October 24, 1983 Dr. Kawaguchi published his famous encyclopedia.
6. 竹田さんはわかいのに白ががあって、目がよく見えなくなっている。
   Even though Mr. Takeda is young, he has gray hair and his eyesight is getting bad.
7. ちょ金ばこから五百円玉を十まい出して、水玉もようのブラウスをかった。
   I took ten ¥500 coins from my piggy-bank and bought that polka dot blouse.
8. 虫が耳の中に入って、くすぐったい。
   A bug went into my ear and it feels ticklish.

9. 土よう日につ雨があけて、ひさしぶりに青空が見えた。

On Saturday the rainy season ended and for the first time in a long time, we could see the blue sky.

10. かれはあさは早く学校へいき、夕がたおそくかえります。

He goes to school early in the morning and comes home late at night.

Quiz 11

A.

1. 日本刀　　2. 丸太　　3. 真弓　　4. 工場　　5. 天才　　6. 十万人　　7. 小刀　　8. 丸一年

B.

1. Japanese archery　　2. carpenter　　3. many talents　　4. fountain pen　　5. short sword, dagger　　6. round face
7. violin bow　　8. workmanship, trick　　9. talent　　10. ¥110,000

C.

1. ぼくとう　　2. だんがん　　3. ゆみや　　4. こうげいひん　　5. あおにさい　　6. ばんざい　　7. しない
8. まるあんき

Quiz 12

A.

1. ひきしお　　2. ぎゅうにゅう　　3. ガスのもとせん　　4. こうべ　　5. ごご　　6. こうがい　　7. ねびき
8. すいぎゅう

B.

1. 元首相　　2. 雨戸　　3. 午前中　　4. 公平　　5. 強引　　6. 牛肉　　7. 元気　　8. 戸外　　9. 正午
10. 公務員

C.

1. 引力　　2. 乳牛　　3. 平成元年　　4. 網戸　　5. 午前　　6. 公言　　7. 値引き　　8. 野牛

Quiz 13

A.

1. this morning　　2. No Parking　　3. young boys and girls　　4. worry　　5. important　　6. the Crown Prince
7. center　　8. prevention

B.

1. e　　2. c　　3. h　　4. f　　5. d　　6. a　　7. i　　8. b　　9. j　　10. g

C.

1. 今月　　2. 中止　　3. 少ない　　4. 心理学　　5. 親切　　6. 太もも　　7. 今日　　8. 止められない

Test Number Four

A.

1. こくない　　2. おとうさん　　3. きぶん　　4. ほうげん　　5. けむし　　6. ともだち　　7. にほんとう
8. にっぽんまる　　9. ようきゅう　　10. こうじちゅう

B.

1. 内田　　2. 神父　　3. 自分　　4. 地方　　5. 友好　　6. 野牛　　7. 五十二才　　8. 万が一　　9. 取引
10. 友人

C.

1. 三分以内　　2. 父方　　3. 十分　　4. 両方　　5. 直毛　　6. 友情　　7. 中元　　8. 神戸　　9. 午前中
10. 公平

D.

1. to look at a guide map　　2. I received ten thousand yen from my uncle.　　3. to ask questions in a direct manner
4. That cow has big, round eyes.　　5. Mayumi is moving (house) today.　　6. to open a door forcefully
7. Park the car where it was before!　　8. to make a story (something) public
9. Now my father is writing characters with a thick brush.　　10. to divide food which is scarce

Answers

E.

1. 私の友だちが心理学をべんきょうしている。
   My friend is studying psychology.
2. 工藤さんに手紙を出そうとおもっていたが、切手が足りなかった。
   I wanted to send Mr. Kudō a letter but I didn't have enough stamps.
3. 毛利さんは四十才になって、少し太りはじめました。
   Mr. Mōri has started to gain a little weight since he turned forty.
4. 白線の内側をあるいて下さい。
   Please walk within the white line
5. 牛は内山さんの方へはしっていった。
   The bull ran towards Mr. Uchiyama.
6. 父が万有引力のほうそくについてはなしてくれた。
   My father explained the law of universal gravitation to me.
7. この電車は川口方めんゆきですか。
   Does this train go to Kawaguchi?
8. 今日の午後友人が田町からくる。
   A friend is coming this afternoon from Tamachi.
9. 公園の水道の水が止まっていたので、ばいてんで牛乳をかった。
   There was no water in the tap in the park, so I bought some milk at the kiosk.
10. 男たちは大きな丸太を引いて、森の中から出てきた。
    The men came out of the forest pulling a large log.

Quiz 14

A.
1. がいむしょう   2. ごきょうだい   3. ふるほんや   4. ひろしま   5. しやくしょ   6. やじるし
7. せきをはずす   8. ちょうけい

B.
1. 古川   2. 広場   3. 朝市   4. 弓矢   5. 外国   6. お兄さん   7. 古寺   8. 背広   9. 市長   10. 吹き矢

C.
1. outward appearance   2. parents and brothers, guardians   3. the classics   4. Help Wanted ad   5. stock exchange
6. shoot back, retaliate   7. go out   8. one's second elder brother

Quiz 15

A.
1. 台所   2. 冬休み   3. 半分   4. 母国語   5. 北海道   6. 使用中   7. 天文台   8. 冬眠

B.
1. はんとう   2. ぼにゅう   3. きたむき   4. きゅうよう   5. やこうしんだいしゃ   6. ふゆやまとざん
7. なかば   8. おかあさん   9. ペキン   10. ひょう

C.
1. lighthouse   2. beginning of winter   3. half portion   4. one's alma mater   5. North Pole   6. use, make use of
7. Taiwan   8. pass the winter

Quiz 16

A.
1. d   2. f   3. b   4. g   5. a   6. e   7. h   8. c

B.
1. きょうかい   2. こうさい   3. こうけい   4. さんこうしょ   5. インコにわ   6. かいしゅう   7. かいぎ
ちゅう   8. こうばん   9. にっこう   10. こうこがく

C.
1. 羽目   2. 今回   3. 会社   4. 交差   5. 栄光   6. 考え過ぎ   7. もう一回   8. 大会

Test Number Five

A.
1. 一方通行   2. 合気道   3. 東大寺   4. 自動車   5. 無色   6. 西村   7. 用事   8. 大会   9. 自宅

10. お兄さん   11. 台本   12. 後半   13. 急行   14. 色っぽい   15. 北西

B.
1. ゆくえ   2. ごうりてき   3. きよみずでら   4. じさつ   5. とくしょく   6. とうざいせん   7. かいけい
8. こっこう   9. しこうりょく   10. だいこう   11. じいん   12. かんさいしんくうこう   13. ないがい
14. ようし   15. しゅうごう

C.
1. a line, queue   2. total   3. mountain temple   4. nature   5. complexion, look   6. Christian Era, A.D.
7. reminisce, reflect on   8. scenery, natural beauty   9. mutual consent, agreement   10. wit and beauty
11. archaeology   12. civic center   13. first day of winter   14. nursery school teacher   15. self-confidence

D.
1. f   2. j   3. g   4. m   5. k   6. c   7. l   8. o   9. a   10. e   11. i   12. b   13. n
14. h   15. d

E.
1. to undo the buttons of a coat   2. Lend me your old comics, will you? (said to an older brother)
3. The fire spread to the north.   4. a red arrow (indicator)   5. I arranged to meet a friend at that old temple
6. I change to winter clothes from about the middle of October.   7. This expression is widely used.   8. This morning I had tests
on classics and chemistry.   9. The color of those shoes doesn't match your clothes.   10. You'd better go yourself.

F.
1. 公園を自転車で二回りした。
    I rode my bicycle twice around the park.
2. デパートの外で矢島さんに会った。
    I met Mr. Yajima outside the department store.
3. その羽かざりの色は白と赤が交じっていた。
    The headdress was a mixture of red and white feathers.
4. 二人は町の広場であいさつを交わした。
    The two people exchanged greetings in the town square.
5. 彼女の目はなみだで光っていた。
    Her eyes were glistening with tears.
6. 少年は自分のこれからの生き方についてよく考えた。
    The youth thought seriously about what kind of life he would lead in the future.
7. 北海道へ行くためのお金が半分たまった。
    I've saved half of the money (I need) to go to Hokkaidō.
8. 母といっしょに市内観光をした。
    I did some sightseeing in the city with my mother.
9. 西村くんのお母さんは台所でおいしそうなケーキをつくっていた。
    Nishimura's mother was making a delicious-looking cake in the kitchen.
10. その白いとりは羽を広げて北西の方へとんでいった。
    The white bird spread its wings and flew off to the north-west.

Quiz 17
A.
1. probably, maybe   2. map   3. reservoir   4. (person) in charge   5. classmate   6. the naked eye
7. majority decision   8. heaven and earth

B.
1. 池田   2. 本当   3. 合同   4. 肉屋   5. 多少   6. 土地   7. 電池   8. 見当   9. 同姓同名   10. 牛肉

C.
1. たはつ   2. ちきゅう   3. いけぶくろ   4. わりあて   5. どうい   6. きんにく   7. ほんだ   8. ちかてつ

Quiz 18
A.
1. 白米   2. 毎朝   3. 何時   4. 三角   5. 汽車   6. 最近   7. 米屋   8. 毎週

B.
1. f   2. d   3. h   4. j   5. g   6. b   7. e   8. i   9. a   10. c

Answers

C.
1. しんまい   2. まいしょくご   3. なんにち   4. こうかくレンズ   5. まいかい   6. せっきん
7. べいこくせい   8. まいばん

Quiz 19

A.
1. triangular shape   2. prediction   3. mountain stream   4. masterpiece   5. society   6. indicate   7. formality
8. a will

B.
1. 渋谷   2. 作文   3. 入社   4. 天気図   5. 人形   6. 言葉   7. 小谷   8. 作品   9. 社長   10. 地図

C.
1. えんけい   2. はつげん   3. だいけいこく   4. さぎょう   5. じんじゃ   6. としょかん   7. けいようし
8. げんごがく

Test Number Six

A.
1. 音声   2. 小走り   3. 大体   4. 弟子   5. 前売り   6. 小麦   7. 低声   8. 地獄   9. 毎日   10. 何時間
11. 本社   12. 地図   13. 方言   14. 毎年   15. 外出   16. 母国   17. 日光   18. 市長   19. 重心
20. 丸太

B.
1. せいたい   2. かっそうろ   3. たいけん   4. とてい   5. うりだしちゅう   6. むぎばたけ   7. うりあげ
8. たよう   9. とうにん   10. にくしん   11. きてき   12. たにま   13. きょうどう   14. まいかい
15. めいげん   16. ようい   17. さんこう   18. こうゆう   19. まわりみち   20. こんかい

C.
1. 大声   2. 脱走   3. 体中   4. 兄弟   5. 安売り   6. 生麦   7. 売店   8. 地方   9. 二百平米
10. 手近   11. 言語学   12. 工作   13. 会社   14. 大麦   15. 体重   16. 古本屋   17. 六時半   18. 北京
19. 社会   20. 矢印

D.
1. e   2. l   3. i   4. t   5. o   6. a   7. q   8. j   9. b   10. s   11. p   12. c   13. k   14. g
15. n   16. d   17. f   18. m   19. r   20. h

E.
1. 小谷さんの犬は池の回りを走っている。
2. 毎日同じライ麦パンのサンドイッチをたべるとあきますね。
3. きみの弟さん、何を作ってるの。 あ、汽車か。
4. はじめて日本に来た友人がおどろいて、「人が多いね」と大声で言った。
5. 「すみません、肉を売っているおみせがこの近くにありますか。」「はい、あそこの角にスーパーがありますよ。」
6. ボールが米山さんの足に当たった。
7. 合図をしたら池のそばの社のところまで走りなさい。
8. 池谷さんの体とわたしの体は同じような形をしている。
9. 西川さんは自分の田んぼでお米を作っている。
10. さく日、うちの近じょでわかい女せいが自さつを図った。

Quiz 20

A.
1. c   2. h   3. f   4. a   5. g   6. e   7. b   8. d

B.
1. らいげつ   2. ばんりのちょうじょう   3. けいかく   4. ようがん   5. けいはん   6. こくれん
7. おねえさん   8. ちじ   9. いらい   10. さとごころ

C.
1. 画家   2. 岩石   3. 東京   4. 国立公園   5. 姉妹   6. 知人   7. 来店   8. 録画

Review Test Two
A.
1. ゆらい　　2. さとおや　　3. まんが　　4. いわやま　　5. きょうだい　　6. こくさん　　7. しまいとし
8. つうち　　9. まるごと　　10. こうぎょう　　11. まんようしゅう　　12. とりひき　　13. ねもと
14. いっこだてのいえ　　15. かんしん　　16. ふるかわ　　17. たいわん　　18. さよう　　19. はねだくうこう
20. かいらん

B.
1. future　　2. foster child　　3. uniform, standard　　4. rock salt　　5. come to Tōkyō　　6. Japanese language
7. companion product　　8. ignorance　　9. business ability　　10. public society, community　　11. pause, suspension
12. decrease, reduction　　13. sword　　14. market conditions　　15. Winter Olympics　　16. peninsula　　17. detour
18. light and heat　　19. selection, choice　　20. great amount

C.
1. 国語　　2. お姉さん　　3. 牛革　　4. 地元　　5. 一切　　6. 外見　　7. 九時半　　8. 北海道　　9. 回り道
10. 交番　　11. 地酒　　12. 池田　　13. 中南米　　14. 毎朝　　15. 水牛の角　　16. 汽車　　17. 付近　　18. 人形
19. 方言　　20. 小谷

D.
1. 日本刀　　2. 弓矢　　3. 午後二時　　4. 正義　　5. 今年　　6. 兄弟　　7. 広島　　8. 台所　　9. 父母
10. 北向き　　11. 急用　　12. 教会　　13. 日光　　14. 多分　　15. 天地　　16. 電池　　17. 本当　　18. 牛肉
19. 米屋　　20. 何日

E.
1. b　　2. g　　3. l　　4. j　　5. a　　6. n　　7. k　　8. r　　9. q　　10. t　　11. f　　12. c　　13. p　　14. s
15. d　　16. i　　17. o　　18. e　　19. m　　20. h

F.
1. e　　2. h　　3. a　　4. l　　5. s　　6. b　　7. k　　8. o　　9. q　　10. c　　11. j　　12. t　　13. d　　14. p
15. r　　16. n　　17. g　　18. m　　19. i　　20. f

G.
1. 「いつとう京に来たのですか。」「今日の午後、姉と一しょに来ました。」
2. 「国はどちらですか。」「中国の北京というところから来ました。」
3. 「岩田くんを知っていますか。」「体が細くて、目が丸くて大きい子ですね。」
4. 村上さんは声が小さくて、今何を言ったか分からない。
5. その古いお寺の近くでお米と大麦をやすく売っているみせがあるそうです。
6. 多分明日母と弟は広しまのへいわきねん公えんを見に行きます。
7. かみの毛を切ってもらって、少ししてから戸谷さんと会った。
8. 今日はもう用がないから、町の池のそばの空き地でキャッチボールをしよう。
9. 羽田からしな川まで、地図を見ないで自てん車で一じかん十分で来られた。
10. 今年の冬のりゅう行の色は黒なので、あなたのような色白の人にはに合うでしょう。

Quiz 21
A.
1. とくちょう　　2. ちょくせん　　3. へいてん　　4. かんとうちほう　　5. しんぽ　　6. しまい　　7. ながねん
8. なかなおり

B.
1. 本店　　2. 中東　　3. 一歩　　4. 直子　　5. 店長　　6. 正直　　7. 売店　　8. 東洋　　9. 歩道　　10. 妹さん

C.
1. one's height　　2. right angle　　3. Middle East　　4. eastern sea, the Pacific　　5. a walk, a stroll
6. sister-in-law　　7. long-term　　8. direct

Quiz 22
A.
1. 明日　　2. 正門　　3. 夜中　　4. 内科　　5. 海外　　6. 生活　　7. 発明　　8. 入門書

B.
1. しんや　　2. きょうかしょ　　3. せとないかい　　4. かつどうてき　　5. せつめいしょ　　6. かどで

Answers

7. やこうれっしゃ　　8. しかい　　9. かいすいよく　　10. かっかざん
C.
1. 証明　　2. 門下生　　3. 白夜　　4. 科学者　　5. 海老　　6. 活力　　7. 不明　　8. 仏門

Quiz 23
A.
1. calculation　　2. the last, the end　　3. puberty, adolescence　　4. greenhouse　　5. party leader
6. clear autumn weather　　7. livelihood, living　　8. latter half

B.
1. 思い出す　　2. 室内　　3. 足首　　4. 秋分の日　　5. 計画　　6. 列の後ろ　　7. 思い出　　8. 寝室　　9. 首輪
10. 秋田県

C.
1. c　　2. e　　3. f　　4. a　　5. h　　6. g　　7. b　　8. d

Test Number Seven
A.
1. 春分　　2. 月食　　3. 火星　　4. 前半　　5. 茶色　　6. 昼夜　　7. 直後　　8. 東北　　9. 合計　　10. 午後

B.
1. 明け方　　2. 水門　　3. 夜行性　　4. 海女　　5. 活気　　6. 春日　　7. 食後　　8. 二人前　　9. 茶目
10. 昼休み

C.
1. Winter nights are long.　　2. to time a race　　3. Please fix this watch immediately.　　4. The dog was eating some food behind the store.　　5. Let's walk while it's still light.　　6. My younger sister was standing in front of the gate.
7. Mr. Akiyama was fired this spring.　　8. An autumn night with twinkling stars　　9. I'd like to go to the seaside tomorrow.
10. That scientist has a tea-ceremony room behind his house.

D.
1. 春日くんは何も知らないのが明らかだ。
   It's clear that Mr. Kasuga knows nothing.
2. えきの東口から出て、時計台まで歩いて下さい。
   Come out of the east exit of the station and walk to the clock tower.
3. お姉さんの赤いセーターの首のところが虫に食われた。
   Moths have eaten holes in the neck of my sister's red sweater.
4. マラソン大会でぼくはみんなに五百メートル後れてゴールインした。ぼくの後ろにはだれもいなかった。
   I crossed the finish line of the marathon five hundred meters behind everyone else. There was no one behind me.
5. 今日の午後の天気予報ははれ後くもりだった。
   The weather forecast for this afternoon said the weather would be fine and later cloudy.
6. 昼も夜も前田くんはいつも教科書ばっかりよんでいるね。
   Maeda reads nothing but textbooks, night and day.
7. 森の中にある小さな石室の近くで東さんと二人で昼食を食べた。
   I had lunch with Mr. Higashi near the small stone hut in the forest.
8. 青森から来た前田くんにとっては東京での学校生活になれるのが大変だった。
   Having come from Aomori, it was difficult for Maeda to get used to school in Tōkyō.
9. 田中さんの妹の年は知っているけれども名前は思い出せない。
   I know Tanaka's younger sister's age, but I can't remember her name.
10. あの年、秋の星空の下で長いあいだあなたと海ぞいのみちを歩いたことを今でもこいしく思っている。
   Even now I still think fondly of that year—those long walks we took along the road by the sea, beneath the starry autumn skies.

Quiz 24
A.
1. 作家　　2. 記入　　3. 十五点　　4. 南北　　5. 春風　　6. 夏時間　　7. 大家　　8. 日記

B.
1. もんだいてん　　2. なんきょく　　3. きょうふう　　4. なつやすみ　　5. せんもんか　　6. きごう
7. しゅうてん　　8. せいなんちほう　　9. ふうしゅう　　10. しょか

C.

1. furniture   2. clearly state, specify   3. Braille   4. south wind   5. first day of summer   6. family   7. record
8. Western style

Quiz 25
A.
1. ふっき   2. げんいん   3. こうきゅう   4. ほうそうし   5. じか   6. いちじかんじゃく   7. ききょう
8. げんりょう

B.
1. high fever   2. photocopy paper   3. speed per hour   4. weak point, weakness   5. return, come home
6. atom bomb   7. maximum, best, great   8. trade journal   9. time difference   10. delicate constitution

C.
1. 帰国   2. 原油   3. 売上高   4. 手紙   5. 時計   6. 弱虫   7. 時々   8. 原寸大

Quiz 26
A.
1. 書道   2. 一方通行   3. 馬車   4. 魚屋   5. 強国   6. 教科書   7. 書店   8. 夜通し

B.
1. d   2. i   3. f   4. a   5. j   6. h   7. c   8. e   9. b   10. g

C.
1. じしょ   2. こうつう   3. たけうま、ちくば   4. きんぎょ   5. きょうちょう   6. きょうし   7. つうち
8. やきざかな

Test Number Eight
A.
1. 黄金   2. 黒人   3. 細川   4. 毎週   5. 雪だるま   6. 船出   7. 黄色   8. 白黒   9. 細工   10. 週日
11. 南極   12. 台風   13. 目白通り   14. 木馬   15. 教会

B.
1. thaw   2. surface mail   3. golden autumn leaves   4. completely black, filthy   5. detailed statement
6. weekly magazine   7. fishing boat   8. blizzard, snowstorm   9. watch, clock   10. hind paw
11. thinking, thought   12. royal family   13. capital city   14. family   15. perfect score, full marks

C.
1. きみ   2. くろじ   3. しょうさい   4. しゅうきゅう   5. なだれ   6. ふうせん   7. きせい   8. かわら
9. こうか   10. わし   11. とうじ   12. きょうじゃく   13. しょるい   14. つうか   15. かぜ

D.
1. c   2. g   3. k   4. e   5. m   6. a   7. h   8. j   9. f   10. o   11. b   12. i   13. n
14. l   15. d

E.
1. The temperature rises when the wind blows from the south.
2. My father's physical condition has gradually deteriorated.
3. to write large characters on white paper
4. My mother taught me oriental calligraphy during the summer vacation this year.
5. Please tell me where the fish market is.
6. A strong-looking man was clearing snow in front of his house.
7. The two of them walk to school in the morning.
8. The tall girl has weak legs so she tires quickly.
9. the Japanese language craze which is gaining popularity overseas
10. Consider your own weaknesses!

F.
1. 今週の火曜日に魚をくわえたねこが家の前を通った。
   On Tuesday this week, a cat passed my house with a fish in its mouth.
2. この黄色い紙に名前を記しなさい。
   Write your name on this piece of yellow paper.

Answers

3. 出来事の細かい話は後にしよう。
   Let's discuss the details of the incident later.
4. お姉さんがガスの火を強めたら、魚が真っ黒にこげた。
   When my sister tuned up the gas, the fish was burnt to a crisp.
5. あの子は足が細くて、色白で、うらやましい。
   I'm envious of her with her slim legs and white skin.
6. 兄は自分の考えを友人に強いた。
   My older brother imposed his will on his friends.
7. 父は子どもの時、米国から中国へ船で行った。
   My father went from America to China by boat when he was a child.
8. 台風の風がまた強まるというので、学校は学生を帰した。
   Since they said the typhoon was gaining strength again, the school sent the students home.
9. 時々、家に帰ってきてから、日記をつけるのをわすれてしまう。
   I sometimes forget to write in my diary after I get home.
10. 子どもたちは原っぱを走り回っている黒い馬を見ていた。
    The children were watching a black horse running around in an open field.

Quiz 27
A.
1. program   2. turkey   3. field, branch   4. cooking   5. rain cloud   6. art exhibition   7. a musical suite
8. swan

B.
1. 上野   2. 理由   3. 雲行き   4. 絵筆   5. 組み立て   6. 小鳥   7. 平野   8. 理解   9. 雲間
10. 絵葉書

C.
1. c   2. e   3. h   4. a   5. g   6. b   7. f   8. d

Quiz 28
A.
1. 時間   2. 場所   3. 秋晴れ   4. 今朝   5. 口答え   6. 北海道   7. 人間   8. 開場

B.
1. 晴雨計   2. 朝市   3. 回答   4. 書道   5. 居間   6. 立場   7. 晴天   8. 毎朝   9. 水道   10. 国道

C.
1. まにあう   2. ばめん   3. はればれ   4. へいあんちょう   5. へんとう   6. ほどう   7. ひるま
8. けいばじょう

Quiz 29
A.
1. d   2. a   3. g   4. h   5. f   6. c   7. e   8. b

B.
1. zoo   2. detour, roundabout way   3. musical instrument   4. renew   5. buying and selling, trade   6. number
7. garden   8. sense of perspective   9. feeling at ease, comfortable   10. fresh

C.
1. 買い物   2. 交番   3. 学園   4. 遠足   5. 音楽   6. 新聞   7. 買い手   8. 一番

Test Number Nine
A.
1. 数学   2. 電力   3. 世話   4. 歌手   5. 中国語   6. 算数   7. 数週間   8. 電光   9. 国歌   10. 語学力
11. 公算   12. 水鳥   13. 雨雲   14. 分野   15. 中間   16. 場合   17. 晴れ間   18. 今朝   19. 道場
20. 番犬

B.
1. たすうけつ   2. でんしこうがく   3. えいかいわ   4. さんびか   5. ものがたり   6. よさん
7. えんちょう   8. ごらく   9. しんぴん   10. そかく   11. とりはだ   12. やさい   13. そうりだいじん
14. うんしゅう   15. あぶらえ   16. たいざいきかん   17. ぼくじょう   18. はれぎ   19. あさごはん

20. かいとう

C.
1. 数字　　2. 電車　　3. 和歌　　4. 外来語　　5. 算出　　6. 人数　　7. 電池　　8. 言語学　　9. 空間　　10. 立場
11. 道理　　12. 売買　　13. 番組　　14. 園田　　15. 気楽　　16. 新人　　17. 山口組　　18. 白鳥　　19. 昼間
20. 電話

D.
1. d　　2. j　　3. t　　4. m　　5. o　　6. a　　7. k　　8 b　　9. r　　10. f　　11. e　　12. p　　13. c
14. i　　15. l　　16. s　　17. n　　18. h　　19. q　　20. g

E.
1. 明日晴れだったら、馬場くんと一しょに日光へ絵をかきに行く。
2. 先週、小学生たちがあの公園の中で楽しく歌を歌っていた。
3. 今、週に二回新しいイタリア語の会話の番組をテレビでやっている。
4. 今朝、雨がふった後だったので、ものすごい数の小鳥が土の中から出て来た虫を食べていた。
5. 遠い雪国へ行った時電車で何時間もかかった。
6. 野口さんは休日にゴルフをして楽しんでいる。
7. 朝起きると雲一つなくて、とてもいい気分になった。それで、ぼくの家の前の道をずっと山まで歩くことにした。
8. 高山先生が話している間に高校生のやく半分がねてしまった。
9. 鳥山くんはその出来ごとを見てきたかのように語った。
10. 元気に歌いながら少年たちは丸太を組んで小やを作った。

Quiz 30
A.
1. どっかいりょく　　2. ふうぶん　　3. らいめい　　4. すいへいせん　　5. おやがいしゃ　　6. せんとう　　7. しらんかお　　8. なんようび

B.
1. 読書　　2. 聞き手　　3. 鳴き声　　4. 電線　　5. 親友　　6. 頭金　　7. 顔色　　8. 水曜日　　9. 訓読み　　10. 外聞

C.
1. e　　2. g　　3.·c　　4. h　　5. d　　6. b　　7. f　　8. a

Review Test Three
A.
1. 読み方　　2. 母親　　3. 新聞　　4. 知らん顔　　5. 日曜日　　6. 店長　　7. 直線　　8. 明かり　　9. 教科書
10. 日本海　　11. 生活　　12. 合計　　13. 後半　　14. 思い出す　　15. 室外　　16. 手首　　17. 秋晴れ　　18. 記入
19. 南風　　20. 時計

B.
1. くとうてん　　2. けんぶん　　3. めいどう　　4. しんかんせん　　5. おやゆび　　6. ずつう　　7. えがお
8. げつようび　　9. てんけん　　10. みなみむき　　11. ふうけいが　　12. きか　　13. げんこう　　14. こうか
15. おりがみ　　16. じさつ　　17. しょさい　　18. てがみいっつう　　19. せんぎょ　　20. べんきょう

C.
1. 読書　　2. 鳴き声　　3. 電線　　4. 親分　　5. 店頭　　6. 顔つき　　7. 何曜日　　8. キリスト教　　9. 組み立て
10. 鳥かご　　11. 上野　　12. 雨雲　　13. 一週間　　14. 歩道　　15. 買い手　　16. 交番　　17. りんご園
18. 遠大な計画　　19. 音楽　　20. 新人

D.
1. Japanese reading of a character　　2. public hearing　　3. resonance, sympathy　　4. wireless, radio　　5. blood relationship
6. brains, head　　7. put to shame, be outdone　　8. Thursday　　9. growth, development　　10. direct(ly), immediate(ly)
11. store employee　　12. walking, a walk　　13. end of rainy season　　14. specialty　　15. last night　　16. encyclopedia
17. seashore, coast　　18. activity　　19. subtotal　　20. later ages, posterity

E.
1. e　　2. h　　3. k　　4. n　　5. r　　6. a　　7. o　　8. s　　9. b　　10. t　　11. q　　12. i　　13. c　　14. g

Answers

15. p   16. d   17. m   18. j   19. l   20. f

F.
1. f   2. n   3. r   4. k   5. s   6. a   7. q   8. j   9. l   10. b   11. p   12. c   13. h
14. m   15. e   16. o   17. i   18. t   19. d   20. g

G.
1. 遠くから歌声がかすかに聞こえてきた。
2. このごろいたずら電話が多くて、頭に来ているよ。
3. 水曜日に親から手紙が来て、すぐに読んで、へんじを出した。
4. ブザーを何回鳴らしても、答えがなかった。
5. 妹がそのおも白い話を聞いた時、顔をまっ赤にして、大声でわらった。
6. さい近、朝、昼、ばん、三回白いごはんを食べている日本人が少なくなってきている。
7. 水平線の少し上につるが三羽とんでいた。そして間もなくまるで黒い点のようになって見えなくなった。
8. 今どは中村さんの読む番だから、よく聞いて下さいね。
9. ドイツ語の教科書の絵ののったページを数えてみたら、十四ページほどあった。
10. 来週の月曜日はお母さんのたん生日だから、きれいな電気スタンドを買ってあげようかな。
11. 公園通りをまっすぐ歩いたら交番につく。書道用のよい紙を売っている店はそのすぐ近くにある。
12. この南のしまは天国みたい！まっ青な海で、空には雲一つなく、夜星がきらきらかがやいていて、国へ帰る気がしない。
13. お寺の門の前に新たにお茶のおいしい店が出来た。
14. 工場のサイレンが正午に鳴ると、昼休みになる。
15. 十月三日のしめ切りに間に合うように、すぐこの場で書いて出して下さい。
16. 黒川さんは新形の自どう車の一ケ月の売り上げがやく六千万円と計算した。
17. おととい親しい友人の園田くんが夏用の黄色いシャツを買ってくれた。
18. 高木さんの家はその細い通りを行って、二つ目の角を右にまがると、すぐ分かると思いますよ。
19. あっという間に風が強くなって、鳥の鳴き声が聞こえなくなった。
20. 週まつに船で遠いしまへ行って、魚つりをして気を晴らした。